The home corner

SU GARNETT

Published by Scholastic Ltd,
Villiers House,
Clarendon Avenue,
Leamington Spa,
Warwickshire CV32 5PR
Text © Su Garnett
© 1996 Scholastic Ltd
1 2 3 4 5 6 7 8 9 0   6 7 8 9 0 1 2 3 4 5

Author
Su Garnett

Editor
Jane Bishop

Assistant Editor
Sally Gray

Series designer
Lynne Joesbury

Designer
Toby Long

Illustrations
Phil Dobson

Cover photograph
Fiona Pragoff

Designed using Aldus Pagemaker
Printed in Great Britain by Hartnolls Ltd,
Bodmin

British Library Cataloguing-in-Publication Data
A catalogue record for this book is available from the British Library.

ISBN 0-590-53639-7

CONTENTS

INTRODUCTION 5

CHAPTER ONE: JEWELLERY SHOP

ALPHABET JEWELLERY 11
DESIGN A NECKLACE 12
PRECIOUS JEWELLERY 13
TREASURE TROVE 14
TWISTERS 15
MIAOW! 16

CHAPTER TWO: TRAVEL AGENCY

WHERE AM I? 17
HOW DID YOU TRAVEL? 18
LET'S CELEBRATE 19
WHERE SHALL WE GO? 20
WE'RE OFF! 21
I GOT RHYTHM! 22

CHAPTER THREE: VET'S SURGERY

PET DIAGRAMS 23
COUNTING RHYMES 24
STROKE GENTLY! 25
LOOK CAREFULLY 26
PETS NEED SPACE 27
MAKING CAGES 28

CHAPTER FOUR: FLOWER SHOP

PETALS 29
ALL SHAPES AND SIZES 30
COMPARING NOTES 31
HOW DO FLOWERS GROW? 32
SUNFLOWERS 33
BEAUTIFUL FLOWERS 34

CHAPTER FIVE: SEASIDE CAFÉ

CAROLINE'S CAFÉ	35
TABLE FOR FOUR	36
GOOD BEHAVIOUR!	37
FEELING HUNGRY?	38
HAVE FUN!	39
BY THE SEASIDE	40

CHAPTER SIX: POST OFFICE

FUNNY STORIES	41
IS THERE ANY POST?	42
HEY MR POSTMAN!	43
HOME SWEET HOME	44
HAPPY BIRTHDAY	45
GUESS WHAT?	46

CHAPTER SEVEN: LIBRARY

BOOKS, BOOKS, GLORIOUS BOOKS!	47
WHERE CAN I FIND IT?	48
ARE YOU SITTING COMFORTABLY?	49
ON, OFF, PAUSE!	50
OUR OWN BOOKS	51
WHAT SEASON?	52

CHAPTER EIGHT: TOY SHOP

LET ME SHOW YOU	53
UP, DOWN OR LEVEL?	54
LET'S PRETEND	55
HIT THE KEYS!	56
WHAT AM I?	57
CAN I PLAY?	58

PHOTOCOPIABLES

DESIGN A NECKLACE	59
WHERE SHALL WE GO?	60
PET DIAGRAMS	61
BEAUTIFUL FLOWERS	62
GOOD BEHAVIOUR!	63
OUR OWN BOOKS	64

Learning through play

The value of constructive play has long been recognised. Learning through play is fun and having fun is conducive to successful learning. The home corner is a vital part of any early learning environment and is seen as somewhere for valuable role-play and social learning to take place. However, in addition, it is possible to achieve successful learning in all six areas outlined by the School Curriculum and Assessment Authority as desirable outcomes for early learning. By providing different locations as settings in the home corner children's learning can be developed in all these areas: Language and Literacy, Mathematics, Personal and Social Development, Knowledge and Understanding of the World, Creative Development and Physical Development.

Setting up the environment

The home corner can literally be a corner of the room, a hinged screen partitioning off an area or a specifically designed house or shop, with a door and windows. You will need to have at least one, preferably more, wall or screen side for display purposes and you will need a reasonable amount of space for the children to move around the area. Involve the children as much as possible in setting up and arranging their new environment.

Keep everything to help create your new environments! All sorts of bits and pieces will be useful. As you assemble and change settings, keep labelled boxes of useful artefacts for future use. At home as you finish the contents of boxes, cartons and bottles, think about their possible use in the play setting. Keep old travel brochures, seed catalogues, telephone directories, postcards, envelopes, clothing, bags and shoes, fabric, bottle tops and so on. Keep small items in large ice-cream containers and the larger ones in cardboard boxes. Label everything carefully and keep one main box for each possible play setting. Ask shops, supermarkets, surgeries, libraries, video shops and publishers for posters and leaflets as appropriate to your chosen setting. Enlist the help of parents and encourage them to contribute things for the group as well.

Health and safety

Throughout this book, reference to safety issues is indicated through the use of the word 'CARE!' where particular care should be taken. Small children are apt to wave things around and often wish to experiment with small items.

In particular take care with:

Scissors: Provide scissors sharp enough to cut but make sure the children carry them carefully (blades down) and never run with them. Make sure they have plenty of room when cutting so they do not accidentally hurt others.

Needles and pins: Children should only be given blunt-ended needles or safety pins but even these can be quite sharp, so ensure adult supervision is provided.

Pipe cleaners: These contain thin wire which can cause injury. Make sure children understand the need to be very careful with them.

Small collage items: Young children love to explore items with their mouths. Ensure they are only given small objects on the strict understanding that they must not put anything in mouths, noses or ears.

Pets: Great care will be needed whenever children come into contact with animals. Any pet can bite or scratch if it is frightened so control any sessions carefully. Remember that some children are allergic to animals.

In addition take care when you move furniture around for new settings; use staplers or staple guns (do not let children handle them); when children are moving around freely and climbing on apparatus and when cooking with the children.

Using adult helpers

Involve the children in setting up your new environments, and enlist adult help to mobilise small groups of children working on different aspects. Once the new environment is established, role-play can be greatly enhanced by adult involvement and direction. The children's knowledge and understanding can be increased and vocabulary skills improved by an adult playing alongside the children.

The role of the adult

An adult working in this way must be very flexible in his or her approach. Sometimes it is best to take a back seat and to watch the children play without intervening. At other times, it is essential to offer quite a lot of help and to be fully involved in the activity. Always be ready to become involved but do not prevent the children from trying things for themselves. In order to draw as much language from the children as possible, always ask open questions. Keep the atmosphere light-hearted and act as naturally as possible with all the children. Never underestimate the children's knowledge, understanding or ability!

Observation and assessment

As children become absorbed in their new setting, it is very easy to watch them at play without being observed. They will feel secure, hidden away in their own 'corner' and their play and behaviour will be very natural. It is easy to observe social skills and to notice how the children interact with one another, who are the natural leaders and so on. Having observed from an inconspicuous position, you may also want to tape conversations by placing the tape recorder in a corner where it is not easily seen. This is very useful for assessing the level of language development in different children and for finding out their level of understanding and interest.

Links with home

Setting up different home corner environments will involve collecting many different items. Ask parents for their help by telling the children what you need. This has the additional benefit that children will go home talking about what they have been doing which will encourage discussion at home. Opportunities may also frequently arise when parents can contribute experiences and memories, as well as artefacts.

How to use this book

This book gives ideas and activities for eight different environments, which are detailed below. Full details of how to set up each scene are provided, ready to start the related activities provided in the book. For each environment there are six activities, one for developing children's learning in each of SCAA's *Desirable Outcomes for Early Learning*. For each activity a suggested group size is given, as well as details of what you need, how to set things up and what to do. It is important to try to make all questions as open-ended as possible, that is, ones which have no specific answer, as this will draw out more ideas from the children. Activities are designed for average four-year-olds, with alternatives for older (five year) and younger (three year) children. Finally, there are some suggested follow-up activities.

The Jewellery Shop

The idea of this shop is to provide the children with a stimulating, exciting environment to explore. Let the children choose bright, shimmering material and pictures of beautiful jewellery from glossy magazines to decorate the shop. Help them to make shop signs and price labels by sticking shiny collage pieces (sequins, shiny sweet papers and foil) onto letter and number shapes. Provide flat surfaces for displaying goods and for a counter where money can be taken. You will also need to provide somewhere where customers can have their sweet wrapper 'stones' (see page 14) set in modelling clay. The shop should have a till, some money, a telephone, and small unbreakable mirrors so that customers can admire themselves wearing various pieces of jewellery before they decide to buy. If possible, make up remnants of velvet into small flat cushions so that precious jewellery can be laid out carefully, for viewing. Provide hooks for necklaces and pendants, thick cardboard tubes for displaying bracelets and flat boxes to arrange brooches in. Ask the children to decorate these boxes and tubes and also small paper bags and tiny boxes for wrapping purchases. Have an area of the shop where you can display jewellery boxes. Fill the shop with as much 'pretend' jewellery as possible, including those made in the activities (see pages 11–16).

The Travel Agency

Decorate the area with postcards from around the world, pictures from travel magazines and, if possible, posters from a real travel agency. Provide two small tables each with two chairs, a telephone, some pads of paper and some pencils. If possible, set up a working computer on one of the desks. Provide plenty of travel brochures and have available old tickets (train, ferry and plane), ticket folders and luggage labels. If possible, add a globe and large maps and atlases.

Before asking children about their holiday experiences be sensitive to any children who may not be as widely travelled as others. Ensure that each child will be able to contribute.

The Vet's Surgery

Hang pictures and photographs of pets on the walls of the surgery. Place leaflets about pets and their welfare in the surgery. Put up signs and compile an index box to put in the Reception as described in 'Pet diagrams' on page 23.

Provide a stethoscope, syringes (without needles) and white overalls (old shirts with the sleeves cut down), small packets and plastic bottles for pretend medicine and pills, together with a white-painted medicine cupboard with a red cross on. Add cages, from the activity, 'Making cages' on page 28, both for keeping the animals before and after 'surgery' and for carrying animals to and from the vet. Have a long table covered with PVC as an operating table. Provide saucers and bottles for pet drinks and bowls for food.

The Flower Shop

Decorate the sides of the shop with paintings and drawings of flowers (see 'Sunflowers' on page 33). Place the big, clay sunflower (from page 33) against the outside wall of the shop. Provide flat surfaces for the till, seed and plant catalogues and for the flowers and plants the children have made (pages 29, 30, 34). Have plenty of flower pots for sale and also small bags of compost and the packets of seeds ('All shapes and sizes' on page 30). Provide another counter for ordering bouquets and buying posies. Put the order book ('Petals' on page 29) on this counter, together with pencils and the gift labels ('Petals' on page 29). You will need a safe shelf or separate table for the real plants ('How do flowers grow' on page 32), flower posies and miniature gardens ('Comparing notes' on page 31).

The Seaside Café

Decorate the walls of the café with a seaside collage (see 'By the seaside' on page 40). Provide two small tables and seven small chairs to set up the café. You will also need enough cutlery, plates, cups and mats for seven people. Provide table-cloths and help the children to make small flower arrangements, either artificial or real. Lay the tables ('Table for four' on page 36) and write out menus ('Caroline's café' on page 35). Have pads and

pencils available for taking orders. Put up welcoming signs ('Caroline's café' on page 35) at the front of the café, together with a striped canopy made out of material or thin card. On one wall of the café, display seaside accessories which are for sale, for example, buckets and spades, little flags, postcards and fishing nets. Add price tags.

The Post Office

Make a large posting box out of a tall cardboard carton painted with bright red gloss paint. Provide two surfaces for counters – one for the shop within the Post Office and one for the counter itself. Make a sign saying 'Post Office' and display leaflets about the various postal services on the walls. Have plenty of cards, postcards, used envelopes and stamps, to sell in the shop, over the counter and also to provide 'post' for the postman's bag. Have other goods for sale – writing paper, local newspapers, tape and string. Make price labels and re-use Post Office bags to wrap goods bought from the shop. Display the wrapping paper and cards ('Happy birthday' on page 45) on a clothes airer, bookshelf or screen. Provide a hat and bag for the postman. Put weighing scales, real 1p coins, pretend postal orders and TV licences on the counter, together with pencils for filling these in. Put all the parcels ('Is there any post?' on page 42) in a hessian sack in the corner of the Post Office.

The Library

Decorate the walls with posters or book covers. (It is worth asking publishers or book suppliers if they have any to spare.) Arrange the inside of the library with comfortable cushions or bean bags. Display the books attractively and have a wide selection on show. Provide a

counter for checking books in and out, together with ink stamps and small cards cut from a large sheet and pencils. Keep an index box with cards showing the children's names and the books they have borrowed. Include a calendar in the Library, showing the day of the week, the date and the month. If your area is big enough, try to group the books into story books, poetry and so on.

The Toy Shop

Put a wide variety of toys, including puzzles, a farm, a garage, a doll's house, bricks, play dough, dolls and teddy bears on shelves or tables in the toy shop. Sort them according to type and display them attractively. If possible, hang dressing-up clothes in one corner of the shop. Put small toys such as marbles and toy cars in sorting trays or decorated cardboard boxes. Make price tags and attach these to items with adhesive tape or safety pins (CARE!). Provide a flat surface for the counter and have play money and a till. Decorate the walls of the Toy Shop with pictures of a variety of toys.

> **Suggestions for other environments:**
> * All kinds of shops – fabric, fruit, bread, shoe, newsagents, hat.
> * Other types of house or different rooms in a house – igloos, lighthouses, kitchen, sitting room.
> * 'People who look after us' settings – doctor's surgery, dentist's, hairdresser's, baby clinic.
> * Different 'museums' and 'art galleries', using the children's work.

LANGUAGE AND LITERACY

Alphabet jewellery, page 11
Where am I?, page 17
Pet diagrams, page 23
Petals, page 29
Caroline's café, page 35
Funny stories, page 41
Books, books, glorious books!, page 47
Let me show you, page 53

THE HOME CORNER

CREATIVE DEVELOPMENT

Miaow!, page 16
I got rhythm!, page 22
Making cages, page 28
Beautiful flowers, page 34
By the seaside, page 40
Guess what?, page 46
What season?, page 52
Can I play?, page 58

PHYSICAL DEVELOPMENT

Twisters, page 15
We're off!, page 21
Pets need space, page 27
Sunflowers, page 33
Have fun!, page 39
Happy birthday, page 45
Our own books, page 51
What am I?, page 57

KNOWLEDGE AND UNDERSTANDING OF THE WORLD

Treasure trove, page 14
Where shall we go?, page 20
Look carefully, page 26
How do flowers grow?, page 32
Feeling hungry?, page 38
Home sweet home, page 44
On, off, pause!, page 50
Hit the keys!, page 56

MATHEMATICS

Design a necklace, page 12
How did you travel?, page 18
Counting rhymes, page 24
All shapes and sizes, page 30
Table for four, page 36
Is there any post?, page 42
Where can I find it?, page 48
Up, down or level?, page 54

PERSONAL AND SOCIAL DEVELOPMENT

Precious jewellery, page 13
Let's celebrate, page 19
Stroke gently!, page 25
Comparing notes, page 31
Good behaviour!, page 37
Hey, Mr Postman!, page 43
Are you sitting comfortably?, page 49
Let's pretend, page 55

Young children have a fascination with bright and shiny objects, such as beads and jewellery. Set up a Jewellery Shop as described on page 7 to provide a stimulating learning environment. Designing necklaces using repeating patterns and exploring the natural properties of pebbles are two of the creative ideas.

ALPHABET JEWELLERY

Learning objective
Language and Literacy – To encourage recognition of letters of the alphabet by shape.

Group size
Up to six children.

Follow-up activities
• Make letter shapes in as many different mediums as possible – dry sand, finger-paint, sewing, painting with water.
• Look at large lettering in magazines. Ask the children to find as many of a particular letter as possible. Do they all look identical?
• Look carefully at signs in the shop. How many letters can the children recognise?

What you need
Self-hardening clay, rolling pins, blunt knives, PVA adhesive, skewer (for adult use only), string, poster paints, lower case 'feely' alphabet letters (made from sandpaper or felt), lower case alphabet frieze.

Setting up
Cover the table with PVC covering. Divide the clay into workable lumps. Provide a small bowl of water to dampen fingers. Place the alphabet frieze within view of the table.

What to do
Start by asking the children to trace over the felt or sandpaper letters with a finger. Make sure they follow the letter shape correctly. Give the correct sound for each letter, asking them to repeat it. Explain that they are now going to make some different letter pendants for the Jewellery Shop. Ask the children to make the letter pendant to match the initial sound of their own name.

Give each child a piece of clay and ask them to roll it into thin snakes which can then be twisted into small letter shapes, imitating the movements made when they traced the 'feely' letters. Check the finished products and help the children correct any wrong shapes. Roll out additional lumps of clay into tiles and press the letters down firmly onto these. (If they fall off when they are dry, they can be glued back on using PVA adhesive.) Before putting the tiles to dry, push the skewer through the top of each tile. When dry, paint and 'varnish' using PVA adhesive. Thread string through the hole in the top to make pendants for the shop.

Questions to ask
What does the clay feel like? What can you make it do? Which letter have you made? Does it look like any other one? Where do we start making this letter?

For younger children
Help younger children to roll out large clay tiles, then draw the outline of letter shapes onto these and invite them to stick pasta shapes or small pebbles onto the clay along the lines of the letters to make their own 'feely' alphabet.

For older children
Ask older children to make upper case letters as well.

DESIGN A NECKLACE

Learning objective
Mathematics – To practice sorting and sequencing.

Group size
Up to eight children.

What you need
Several old necklaces or bracelets, beads of different shapes, sizes and colours, dry pasta for threading, small squares of different coloured shiny paper, blunt-ended needles, embroidery thread, scissors, modelling clay, sorting trays.

Setting up
Provide each child with sorting trays and a selection of items with which to make their jewellery. Give each child a needle threaded with a knotted thread and a small lump of modelling clay.

What to do
Show the children examples of ready-made jewellery and help them to identify sequences within these, such as two green beads, one gold, two green and so on. Next ask the children to sort items for threading, bearing in mind type, colour, size and shape. Explain that they are going to make their own necklaces to sell in the Jewellery Shop. Before they start to thread make sure they understand how their sequence will work. Tell them to start threading with a square of paper, to provide a base for their designs. If the children experience difficulty when threading, especially when trying to make holes in the paper, suggest that they lay the paper on a lump of modelling clay and push the needle down into it.

When the necklace is long enough, slip the designs along the thread a little to free the paper end. Then tie both ends of the thread together and cut off neatly.

Questions to ask
Can they explain their sequence? What comes next? Why? Who is this necklace for? How long will it need to be? Who has beautiful jewels like these? What do you feel like when you wear jewels?

For younger children
Use commercially available material to practise sequencing patterns – such as chain links or snap-together beads.

For older children
Help the children to make sequences using coloured paper clips, by sliding these together to join them into a chain. Another possibility is to help them to make paper chains using ready-made adhesive paper strips.

Follow-up activities
• After a 'play' session in the shop, encourage the children to tidy up by sorting the goods in the shop into groups or 'sets' of necklaces, bracelets, brooches and so on.
• Use the photocopiable sheet on page 59 to practise sequencing.
• Draw the children's attention to repeating patterns on fabric or wallpaper as well as other sequence patterns we encounter all the time – day following night, days of the week, months and seasons.

PRECIOUS JEWELLERY

Learning objective
Personal and Social Development – To encourage the children to treat property with care and respect.

Group size
Up to eight children.

What you need
Examples of jewellery and jewellery boxes. Aim to show the children a wide range of jewellery, including intricate metal work and heavily beaded examples. If parents are willing, ask them to bring in and show some precious things, or if they send items in with the children make sure you have somewhere safe to keep them.

Setting up
Explain to the children that they are going to share their precious things with each other. Point out that they would all be sad if items were broken and make sure that they understand the need to handle everything with great care. Sit in a large circle where everyone can see clearly.

What to do
Encourage the children to take it in turns to talk about their precious jewellery. Children who are watching will be very anxious to see and handle the jewellery and it is a very good test of patience to have to wait and take turns. Make it very clear, by your own example, how you expect the children to treat this special property. Let children take a reasonable length of time to examine items but make sure they all sit and listen carefully. Explain that special items need special care and show the jewellery boxes to the children, telling them that these are places to store valuable items. Examine these carefully and notice any common features.

Questions to ask
Who gave you this? When? Why? Was it a special present for a special occasion? How do you look after your special things? What other things are precious to you?

For younger children
Have a smaller group of only four children so that the items can be seen more clearly and the children don't have to wait so long to examine things.

For older children
If appropriate – and this has to be at your discretion – make this an opportunity to discuss stealing. Why is it wrong to take something that doesn't belong to you?

Follow-up activities
• Make some jewellery boxes out of reclaimed materials to place in your jewellery shop.
• With the children, draw up a list of rules for looking after the various items of jewellery they have all made for the shop. How will they ensure these do not get lost or broken?
• Talk about feelings? What makes the children sad/angry?

TREASURE TROVE

Learning objective
Knowledge and
Understanding of the
World – To explore the
features of natural
stones and pebbles.

Group size
Up to eight children.

What you need

Dull-looking stones of different sizes (from the garden or hillside), pebbles of serpentine or other pretty stones. Encourage both adults and children to bring in examples of crystals, semi-precious stones, cut-in-half stones or minerals which they may have collected or bought from museums and shops. A small bowl of water. Pictures of precious and semi-precious stones, set in rings, necklaces, earrings and brooches.

Setting up

Sit the children in a large circle, so that they can all see clearly.

What to do

Ask the children if they know where beautiful jewels come from. Explain that they start off as dull stones buried in rocks high up in the mountains and at the bottom of rivers (show some examples). They will probably not see any similarity between the dull stones and sparkling rings, so demonstrate how dry serpentine pebbles are transformed when they are put into water. Show them the patterns and veins in the rock and how beautiful they look.

Tell the children that sparkling jewels are not made by putting dull stones into water but by cutting them with a special machine, so that the light shines off them. Now look at some of the sparkling jewellery you have made for your shop. Decorate the shop walls with pictures of real jewellery cut from glossy magazines.

Follow-up activities
• Help the children to make 'precious stones' by screwing up shiny sweet wrappers into tiny balls. Offer a stone setting service in the shop where the children can choose a 'stone' to set in modelling clay.
• Have any children seen the Crown Jewels? Show them photographs of all the beautiful jewels in these and display these photographs in the shop.
• Visit a museum with a Geology department, to look at precious stones in both their natural and cut state.

Questions to ask

Do you know the names of any of these jewels? How do you think the stones which become jewels are removed from the rocks? Show them that jewels are often set in metal. Do you know which metals are used?

For younger children

Take a walk outside and let the children find soft grass and muddy patches and compare these with the hard surfaces of tarmac, stones and cement. Emphasise that jewels are only found inside hard rock, usually up in mountains.

For older children

Make a simple papier mâché island, showing several geographical features – rivers, sea, mountains and low-lying areas. Where do they think they would find treasure?

TWISTERS

Learning objective
Physical Development
– To practise handling
small objects with
increasing control.

Group size
Four children.

What you need
A selection of long coloured pipe cleaners (CARE!), three long scarves in different colours, adhesive tape.

Setting up
Tie the three scarves together at one end and plait them. Let the children watch what you do, encouraging close observation.

What to do
Ask the children to choose three pipe cleaners in different colours. Tell them not to point pipe cleaners near faces as they may have sharp ends. Explain that they are going to make these into bracelets to wear and sell in the Jewellery shop. Tape the pipe cleaners side-by-side to the table surface in front of them. Help the children to make the pipe cleaners up into plaits, pulling each one over reasonably tightly so that the result is a neat plait. Emphasise the need for careful concentration while doing this, to make sure the plait is formed correctly.

When the plait is long enough to go round their wrist, allowing sufficient room for slipping over their hand, remove the tape holding the pipe cleaners to the table and help the children to twist the ends together to form a bracelet. Display the bracelets in the shop.

Questions to ask
Ask questions as they work: Which colour do we need to use next? What do we do with this pipe cleaner to continue the plait? Can you see the plait beginning to form? Have you seen plaits before? Where? What else could we make with plaits? (Pet collars and leads, book marks, hair bands.)

For younger children
Instead of plaiting, let the children twist two pipe cleaners together to make bracelets.

For older children
Try experimenting with other materials for making plaits, for example thick wool or coloured string. This time, it is probably easier to tie the ends together before taping to the table.

Follow-up activities
• At Christmas, plait different coloured tinsel to decorate the Jewellery shop.
• What is inside pipe cleaners? Talk about the bendy properties of wire and the stretchiness of wool.
• Encourage children to use play apparatus and to move in ways which will reinforce the language which has been demonstrated while plaiting, for example; over, under, between and next to.
• Talk about hairstyles. Do any children with long hair have plaits? Produce a block graph of different hairstyles such as, plaits, fringes and pony tails.

MIAOW!

Learning objective
*Creative development –
To use a selection of
materials to represent
a familiar pet.*

Group size
Up to six children.

What you need
Thick card of different colours, adhesive tape, PVA adhesive, Velcro, a selection of items for collage work (CARE!) for example, dry pasta of different shapes and sizes, small beads and pebbles, buttons, drinking straws, used matchsticks, wool, string, felt, fabric remnants, sequins, foil, card. Photographs of cats.

Setting up
Cut circles with eight centimetre diameters from the thick card. Give each child a circle in the colour of their choice, together with a pot of adhesive and a brush. Spread out all the collage items in separate trays so that they are readily accessible to all the children.

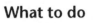

What to do
Explain that the children are going to make cat brooches to sell in the shop. Look together at photographs of cats and discuss features such as eyes, ears and whiskers. Encourage the children to select items from the collage material which remind them of a cat's face. Ask them to arrange their collage pieces on the card circle and when they are satisfied with the design, to stick this on to the card, using the PVA adhesive. Help them to cut fabric and card as necessary. When the faces are dry, stick a piece of Velcro to the back to make a brooch. Display these in the shop for the children to buy and wear.

Questions to ask
Do you have a cat at home? What do her eyes look like? Do you think these buttons/sequins/beads look like her eyes? Why? Have you felt her whiskers? What do they feel like? Is her nose cold/wet? What can we find from these bits which reminds us of her nose? What are her ears like? Can we find something like them?

For younger children
Mark the card circles to show where eyes, mouth, nose, ears and whiskers should go. Have a more limited selection of collage pieces, together with pre-cut ears.

For older children
Ask them to mix powder paints, to produce 'cat' colours and paint the background before adding collage pieces.

Follow-up activities
• Examine how Velcro works and when using the brooches notice how the hooks cling onto material. Does it stick more easily onto certain clothes?
• Make a giant-sized brooch, twenty centimetres in diameter. Look at the shapes involved – circle face, oval eyes with diamond middles, rectangle mouth, triangle ears and nose, cylinder whiskers. Compare this with the small brooches.

TRAVEL AGENCY

Children's natural enthusiasm for different types of transport and making journeys can be developed in the setting of a Travel Agency. See page 7 for how to set the scene. Children are encouraged to talk about their own experiences and can learn about festivals and music around the world as well as taking part in recording the results of a simple travel survey.

WHERE AM I?

Learning objective
Language and Literacy – To listen to and talk about the children's holiday experiences.

Group size
Up to eight children.

What you need
Ask each child to bring in a few photographs of themselves on holiday (preferably away from home).

Setting up
Sit everyone in a large circle, with their photographs, so that everyone can see clearly.

What to do
Start by explaining that they are all going to take turns to show the group some photographs of themselves on holiday. Encourage each child to tell the group who is in their photograph, when and where it was taken, what they are doing and whether they enjoyed being there. Ask them to give as much useful information as possible about different locations and types of holiday, different climates, landscapes, local wildlife and so on. When all the children have shared their information, add to the discussion and understanding of the group by sharing some of your own experiences and photographs, using material collected for the 'Travel Agency'.

Questions to ask
Try to ask open-ended questions to encourage further discussion. For example: Why are you wearing a swimsuit? Why are all the houses white? What can you see that is different to our town/country? Why are you wrapped so warmly?

For younger children
Encourage close observation of the photographs in a smaller group and identify types of holiday. For example, winter and summer ones, those at the seaside, in the country and in the town.

For older children
Encourage comparison of two different holidays, using their photographs. Which did they enjoy more and why? Which did they find more exciting?

Follow-up activities
• Role-play a holiday situation. Let the children decide where they will be going and make all the necessary preparations, including visiting the Travel Agency.
• Pack a case with dressing up clothes, suitable for going on holiday.
• Let the children take it in turns to be information givers and seekers in the Travel Agency. Be prepared to offer help where necessary to increase the value of the play.
• Invite other adults into your group to show photographs and to share their holiday experiences.

HOW DID YOU TRAVEL?

Learning objective
Mathematics – To practise recording information using a block graph.

Group size
Whole group.

What you need
Register books, large pieces of squared paper, coloured felt-tipped pens, large sheets of card, scissors, adhesive.

Setting up
Sit the children in small groups at tables. Give each child several square pieces of paper (approximately 2 x 2cm, cut from the large pieces of paper) and some felt-tipped pens.

What to do
Talk about different ways of recording information. Take a register of the group and let the children watch you as you mark off each name. Help one child to count the marks and explain that this tells us the number of children in the group today. Reinforce the concept that one mark stands for one child. Explain that they are going to make a record of how many children have been in cars, ferries, aeroplanes, trains and so on.

Ask them to think about any holidays they have had. Then take each form of transport in turn and ask the children to put up their hands if they have been in or on it. Include a few unusual ideas as well (such as a hot air balloon) to check that children are not just saying yes to everything! For every form of transport they have been in, ask the children to colour in one of their squares. Help the children cut out their squares. Mark out several columns on the card, with pictures of cars, trains and so on at the base of the column. Then let the children stick their squares in the appropriate column. Show the children the finished graph, explaining that the different heights of the columns show the number of children who have used the various forms of transport.

Questions to ask
How many children have been in, for example, cars? Which column is the tallest/smallest? So, which form of transport have most/least children been in? Are any columns the same height? What does this mean?

For younger children
Instead of colouring squares, let younger children make a three-dimensional block graph, using building blocks, choosing different coloured blocks to represent the different forms of transport (one with a picture on the front to remind the children).

For older children
In pairs, let them make their own graph. Give them a small piece of squared paper already divided into columns. One child should conduct the survey of their friends, while the other should colour in one square of the appropriate column for each positive answer.

Follow-up activities
• Hang the finished graph in the Travel Agency and conduct a similar survey amongst any visitors.
• Record the information gathered in sets. Draw large circles on sheets of paper, adding writing and pictures – one for each form of transport. Children draw pictures of themselves in the appropriate sets. Compare this with the original graph. Which is easier to 'read'?

LET'S CELEBRATE

Learning objective
Personal and Social Development – To develop an awareness of cultural and religious events around the world.

Group size
Up to eight children.

What you need
Following special festivals, for example Christmas, Eid-ul Fitr (the end of the fast of Ramadan), Chinese New Year, Holi, Easter and so on, ask the children to bring in any related items including their own photographs of themselves with families or friends at these celebrations. (For extensive explanation of the various festivals throughout the world see *Bright Ideas for Early Years: Festivals and Celebrations* (Scholastic) and *Bright Ideas: Festivals* (Scholastic).)

Setting up
Sit everyone in a large circle, with their photographs, so that everyone can see clearly.

What to do
Let the children take turns to speak and ask the children to listen carefully. Draw out information by encouraging each child to tell you when this festival occurs – month and season if possible – and what they do to celebrate. Do they have people to stay at their home or do they travel to families and friends? Discuss all the preparations involved to get ready for the event and encourage children with particular knowledge and different experiences to contribute as fully as possible. Discuss whether they dress up, dance, eat special food, decorate the house, buy or give presents and so on. End the session by looking together at the significance behind these celebratory events, for example, the birth of Jesus, the beginning of a new year, or a thanksgiving for the harvest.

Questions to ask
Looking at the photographs ask: How many members of your family are here? How are they related to you? What do you remember most about these occasions? What is the longest journey you have made to be with your family or friends at these special times?

For younger children
To help them to remember and to maintain interest, look at some of their presents or clothes associated with these events as a basis for productive discussion.

For older children
Encourage these children to give individual or small group performances of dances, songs or customs associated with these events, for example two children could decide what New Year's resolutions they are going to make.

Follow-up activities
• Role-play journeys undertaken at these times. Pretend to make arrangements with family or friends and book tickets at the Travel Agency.
• Cook some celebratory foods – mince pies (Christmas), apples dipped in honey (Rosh Hashanah – Jewish New Year) and Barfi (Raksha Bandhan – Hindu festival of caring).
• Stage an event for your parents to enjoy, for example a Harvest Festival or a Chinese dragon dance.
• To celebrate Diwali (October/ November), decorate the play house with rangoli patterns and small candles made from cardboard rolls and tissue flames, to imitate diva lamps.

WHERE SHALL WE GO?

Learning objective
Knowledge and Understanding of the World – To begin to recognise some of the features of different areas of the world.

Group size
Up to six children.

What you need
A wide selection of travel brochures, calendars, books, posters and postcards showing different areas of the world. Invite the children to provide anything they can.

Setting up
Sit the children around a large table and spread the brochures and pictures out in front of them.

What to do
Let the children select a brochure to look at, and give them time to browse through the pages to find their favourite pictures. Encourage them to look carefully at the details pointing out the sky, beach, sea, flowers, mountains and rivers. Let each child describe their picture. Can they guess from the picture whether it is a hot or cold country? Tell them the name of the place they are looking at and which country it is in. Together, find out where the country is on the globe. In relation to Great Britain, where is it and is it a big or small place? Is it surrounded by sea or land?

Questions to ask
What do you like about this picture and why would you like to be there? How is it different from where you live? How could you arrange to go there?

For younger children
Restrict brochures and pictures to those that might particularly appeal to this age group (seaside locations/showing animals) and encourage them to look carefully at the geographical features of these areas too.

Follow-up activities
• Discuss how to reach various places. Do you have to go over blue areas (sea) from Great Britain to get there? Would you go by ferry or aeroplane? Could you go by train? Use the photocopiable sheet on page 60.
• Sort brochures in the Travel Agency into Summer and Winter holidays, holidays for children, holidays by the seaside and so on.
• Encourage the children to familiarise themselves with the brochures in the Travel Agency. Can they find the right one to give a customer wanting a safari holiday or one to Disneyland?

For older children
How many geographical features can the children identify in their various pictures? Talk about fresh and salt water and different amounts of water in streams, ponds, rivers, lakes, channels and oceans. Discuss hillocks, hills and mountains and sandy beaches and deserts. Looking at the globe, identify islands.

WE'RE OFF!

Learning objective
Physical Development – To use large play equipment with confidence.

Group size
Up to eight children.

What you need
Several large, wheeled toys such as tricycles and scooters. Other large play equipment which can be adapted to different uses, some with wheels (steering, if possible) and some without. Climbing frames, low benches and PE mats.

Setting up
Use a room with plenty of space for the children to move around. Spread out the play equipment and make sure that two adults keep a careful watch to avoid collisions and tumbles. (CARE!)

What to do
Encourage the children to use their imaginations – ask them to imagine that they are going on holiday to various destinations by car, train, ferry or plane. Watch as they use the equipment in various ways, offering help and ideas where necessary. Encourage them to use parts of their bodies, as well as the equipment. Help them to improve their skills by repeating climbing and balancing exercises. Suggest that the sea is very rough as the ferry crosses to France and that they must balance carefully to avoid falling over. The climbing frame is a very useful piece of equipment for imaginative flights. As the aeroplane takes off, children can climb up the frame, coming down the slide as it comes in to land. Set up an imaginary road with bends, traffic lights and zebra crossings. Using the wheeled toys, increase the children's manipulative skills by making them stop, slow down and go round corners.

Questions to ask
Where are you going? Who is coming with you? How do cars and trains know when they must stop? How can cars and trains go over water? (Bridges, ferries.)

Follow-up activities
- Buy tickets from the Travel Agency for their imaginary journeys.
- Try to arrange a visit to an adventure playground so that the children can practise their improved co-ordination skills.
- Discuss other means of transport. Can they think of animals who are used to carry things around?
- Make traffic lights by painting circles of red, orange and green to mount on a wooden stand. Use these for imaginative play.

For younger children
Role-play a journey, using the various pieces of apparatus. For example, drive to the airport in the car, get into a train to the terminal and then in an aeroplane. End the journey with a drive to your hotel.

For older children
Let the children set up an obstacle course for themselves, pretending they are 'stunt' cars. Try to have slopes to zoom up and down, sharp bends to negotiate, chasms to leap over and tunnels to whizz through.

I GOT RHYTHM!

Learning objective
Creative Development
– To respond to
rhythm in music and
dance.

Group size
The whole group.

What you need
Examples of instruments and recorded music from different countries, for example steel bands, Indian music, African drums, Greek music, Scottish dance music and Spanish castanets.

Setting up
Use a room with plenty of space for the children to move around. Spread out all the instruments carefully so that the children can see them without risk of damage.

What to do
Explain that you are going to listen to the sounds of instruments from other countries. Identify where each instrument comes from and let the children look carefully at the instruments. If possible invite someone in to play them and make sure the children hear each instrument individually. Follow this initial exploration by encouraging the children to dance and sway to the various types of music suggested above. Let them make up their own movements according to whatever the music suggests to them. Watch a video of cultural dancing at festivals such as Mardi Gras and Holi if possible as this would add to their understanding and enjoyment.

Questions to ask
Which sound do you like best? When you have visited other countries, have you watched people dancing to local music? Does the music make you want to move?

For younger children
Introduce some dressing-up clothes, for example saris, clogs and flowing scarves, to add to the children's enjoyment when moving around.

For older children
Teach older children a simple country dance to perform to Scottish dance music, to increase their co-ordination skills.

Follow-up activities
• Encourage the children to look through the travel brochures to find pictures of cultural dancing. Look at the clothes which are worn.
• Make a grass skirt to use when dancing and to hang in the Travel Agency as a decoration. Stick lengths of raffia onto a waistband of wide masking tape. Cover the ends with another band of tape on the top. Join the two ends with Velcro.
• Try making rhythm drums by stretching different materials, for example, thick polythene, greaseproof paper, foil and cotton fabric, tightly over small, rigid containers. Which makes the most realistic sound?
• Ask the children to repeat rhythms which you tap out on drums or castanets by tapping their fingers on the table.

CHAPTER THREE

Projects involving pets and animals are always popular with young children. Set up a Vet's Surgery as described on page 8, to provide an opportunity for children to show concern for living things. With these activities children are encouraged to learn about pets in a variety of ways, such as through rhymes and songs and by carefully designing cages for pets.

PET DIAGRAMS

Learning objective
Language and Literacy – To practise writing skills, using writing for labelling.

Group size
Up to eight children.

What you need
Photocopiable page 61, one for each child. Pencils and erasers.

Setting up
Give each child a pencil, eraser and a photocopied sheet. Explain that they are going to label the cat in the picture to show what each part is called; say that this is called a diagram.

What to do
Using a large picture or photograph from the display in the Vet's Surgery examine the different parts of the cat's body. Identify whiskers, paws, claws, nose, ears and fur. Then tell each child to look carefully at the words printed on the sheet. Ask, if by looking at the first letters of the words and their sounds, they can tell which word says 'whiskers'? Having identified

each word, help them to cut them out and stick them in the correct places. Finally encourage them to copy the word on the line underneath. Finish by asking each child to colour in their cat.

Questions to ask
What sound does this letter make? (Pointing to the *p* of 'paws'). So which word do you think says 'pppp...aws'? Where should you start writing this letter? Now where do you go? Are you holding your pencil properly? Why do we label things? Can you think of other things we might label and why?

For younger children
Help the children to look at letter sounds in the following way. For example, *c* says 'cccc' so we should put this word by something in the diagram beginning with 'cccc' – his claws. Rather than copying the whole words practise writing first letters only.

For older children
Some older children will be able to identify the correct words and copy them straight on to the line without any help. Encourage those who feel able to do this. For those who are less confident, try to develop independent thought by giving them sufficient time to think before you offer help.

Follow-up activities
• Ask the children to write signs for the surgery – waiting area, operating room and reception.
• Keep an index box with the names and addresses of pet owners who visit the surgery.
• Write a letter to a friend describing their excitement about a new pet.
• Explain some of the uses of writing, giving directions (the surgery signs), keeping information (the index box of names and addresses) and giving pleasure (writing letters to friends).

COUNTING RHYMES

Learning objective
Mathematics – To practise counting activities through rhymes and songs about pets.

Group size
Whole group.

What you need
The words of several rhymes and songs involving pets. A clear voice and plenty of enthusiasm!

Setting up
Sit the children in a large circle around you.

What to do
Start with a song that the children are all likely to know, for example 'Five little ducks went swimming one day.' Recite the rhyme with the children, pausing so that they fill in the numbers. Continue with several other songs and rhymes, such as: 'Two little dicky birds'; 'One, two, three, four, five, once I caught a fish alive'; 'One elephant went out to play'; 'Five little monkeys walked along the shore' (Anon (in *Tiny Tim* by Jill Bennett and Helen Oxenbury, Mammoth); 'Baa, baa black sheep'; 'I think mice are rather nice' (by Rose Fyleman in *Tiny Tim* by Jill Bennett and Helen Oxenbury, Mammoth).

Every time you encounter numbers, let the children fill in the gaps. If you choose your rhymes carefully, for example, finding one more each time or losing one each time, the children will be introduced to simple oral addition and subtraction. With practice and constant repetition, the children should become quite adept at number order and the basic concept of addition and subtraction.

Questions to ask
Can you tell me how many (animals) we have this time? If one flies away now, how many will we have? Which is the biggest/smallest number – one or ten? Which is the most/least – one or ten? Can you count the numbers in order from one to ten? Can you say the order of numbers, backwards, from ten to one? If one more comes/goes will the total number of pets be bigger or smaller?

For younger children
While singing songs and saying rhymes, encourage the children to either act out the part of the pets coming and going or use toy animals to coincide with the correct numbers in the rhymes and songs. This should help to reinforce their learning.

For older children
Invite the children to devise their own rhymes and songs, perhaps using a familiar tune, such as 'Ten green bottles'. For example: Ten fluffy kittens sitting on the mat, Ten fluffy kittens sitting on the mat, And if one fluffy kitten should grow into a cat, There'd be nine fluffy kittens sitting on the mat.

Follow-up activities
• Using the pictures, books and photographs in the Vet's Surgery, encourage the children to count accurately: numbers of claws on pet's feet; whiskers on faces; spots on fur.
• Put this rhyme up outside your surgery;
'Do you have a dog or cat?
Is he thin or much too fat?
If you bring him to the vet
You will keep a healthy pet.'
• Begin to solve practical problems such as: We have four pets. How many cages will we need?
• Use different mathematical language; more, less, spend, grow, heavy, and so on.

STROKE GENTLY!

Learning objective
Personal and Social Development – To treat living things with care and concern.

Group size
Two children.

What you need

If your group has a pet, this can be carefully examined. If not, ask a parent to bring in a pet which the children could carefully handle. (CARE!) It is essential that the pet is good-natured and trustworthy. Provide a quiet corner in the room and only allow two children near the animal at any one time. Protective covering for the floor is also a good idea!

Setting up

Sit two children in the vet's surgery which must be very quiet for the duration of this activity. Bring in the group pet in its cage, or an imported pet, with its owner. Sit down close to the children.

What to do

Having taken any specific advice from the pet's owner, very carefully and gently, give one child the pet to hold and stroke, (if it is small enough to handle). Otherwise, encourage the children to approach the pet slowly while it is sitting with its owner. Encourage gentle stroking in the direction of the lie of the fur and very careful handling so that the pet does not get squeezed too tightly. Discourage violent actions, too much noise or over-excitement, always explaining why this is not a good idea. Talk to the owner about how they look after the pet. What does it like to eat and drink? How do they keep it clean? If it is unwell, what do they do? How do they show the pet that they are fond of it? How do they know if the pet is frightened? Invite the children to contribute their own knowledge as well so that the discussion becomes a genuine dialogue.

Questions to ask

Do the children have pets? What do they have? Why do we have to stroke and handle pets so gently, especially very small ones?

For younger children

Only handle pets in a one-to-one situation and emphasise even more strongly the need for caution. Do not place pets into the children's hands but let them stroke the animal while you or the owner holds it.

For older children

Encourage older children to handle and stroke the group pet as they clean its cage or change its food as this will reinforce both the pleasure and the responsibilities involved in having a pet. If a pet is brought in, perhaps it could be brushed, under supervision, or some other aspect of its care undertaken.

Follow-up activities
• Let the children look after pretend 'pets' in the Vet's Surgery. Take it in turns to be vet and owner. If possible, invite someone in to the group who can show the children some unusual 'pets', from different parts of the world.
• Invite a vet or veterinary nurse to come and talk to the children about their work.

LOOK CAREFULLY

Learning objective
Knowledge and
Understanding of the
World – To talk about
their observations of
pets, noting similarities
and differences.

Group size
Up to six children.

What you need
Several detailed pictures of domestic pets (include dogs, cats, rabbits, guinea-pigs, hamsters and budgies). Explanatory books about the lives and needs of these animals, with close-up photographs. Use pictures, photographs and pamphlets from the Vet's Surgery.

Setting up
Sit the children around a big table. Spread out a selection of the books and pictures on the table.

What to do
Ask the children to look very carefully at the pictures and photographs. Give each child a specific animal to study and make sure they find all the pictures and photographs for that particular animal. Encourage them to look carefully at the various features of that animal, including eyes, noses, ears, feet/paws, whiskers and so on. After a while, compare notes. You will need to act as referee, making sure that each child is fairly heard and that important observations, including similarities and differences, are noted by others in the group. Which animals have fur, feathers and hair? How many different kinds of feet/claws/paws have they seen?

Follow-up activities
• Encourage the children to paint and draw some pictures of the animals to hang in the Vet's Surgery.
• Put a large photograph of a human face next to the pictures of pets in the surgery. Discuss the differences between the features of pets and our features.
• Copy animals and try walking on all fours. Can the children move very quickly like a dog?
• Examine some feathers. Notice how they stick together and how water rolls off them, to keep birds dry.

Questions to ask
Can they tell which animals are awake at night time? (Large eyes so they can see in the dark.) In the dark, we find it difficult to find our way around without bumping into things. Some animals are much better at this. Why? (They have very good hearing and use their whiskers as an indication of how close they are to things.) How do cats keep their claws sharp? How do dogs drink? Do rabbits drink in the same way?

For younger children
Limit the animals to dogs, cats, rabbits and guinea-pigs. Ask them to look at how the animals move and what noises they make as well as the features suggested above.

For older children
Having made the observations suggested, make a chart (using pictures) to show which animals have whiskers, claws, paws, fur, hair, feathers and so on.

PETS NEED SPACE

Learning objective
Physical Development
– To develop an
awareness of space
and other people.

Group size
Whole group.

What you need
A large hall or room with plenty of space to move around.

Setting up
Most children will probably have been to zoos or safari parks and many will have their own pets. They may well have some idea of how animals feel in small and large spaces. However, in order to increase that understanding, explain to the children that they are going to experience, for themselves, what it feels like to move around in lots of space and in contrast, a very restricted space.

What to do
Establish some ground rules! Tell the children they will be able to move around freely but they must move carefully, all in the same direction, not too fast. Agree signals for 'start' and 'stop' and make sure these signals are adhered to (CARE!). At first, allow the children to use the whole of your available space. Watch carefully as they enjoy the freedom and space. Gradually decrease the available space by shutting off part of the room with chairs. As the space gets smaller, you will notice more frustration amongst the children. Others may well get in their way, preventing them from doing what they want to. Even if they try to get out of each other's way, this may be difficult. Use your discretion to control how long each session should last and be ready to step in to stop any potential collisions. As the space gets very small, nearly all movement will cease as there is simply no room for anyone to move independently. Open up the space again and sit the children down to assess the experience.

Questions to ask
How did you feel when you had lots of space? What was it like trying to move in less space? Did you like having other people close around you all the time? What do you think pets feel like if they are kept in very small cages? How do you think they feel if they never have a chance to run around freely? How can you ensure your pet is kept happy?

For younger children
Control the session more rigidly, asking for specific movements in the various environments. For example, running on tiptoe, turning around and lying on the floor.

For older children
When the space gets very cramped, how can the children give themselves a little more room? (By tensing up their bodies, putting arms close by their sides.) Does this feel nice?

Follow-up activities
• Look at the cages in the surgery. Do the pets have sufficient space to move around?
• Encourage role-play in the surgery. The vet can ask whether the pet is getting enough exercise.
• Play games, such as musical bumps and statues to practise making the most of the available space without bumping into others.
• In a group, try balancing on one leg in a confined space without leaning over onto other people.

MAKING CAGES

Learning objective
Creative Development
– To encourage use of
imagination in the
design of pet cages.

Group size
Up to four children.

What you need
Several large, strong cardboard boxes, a range of fabrics, thick string, upholstery needle and craft knife (for adult use only), pipe cleaners, treasury tags, modelling clay, twigs, poster paint, palettes, brushes.

Setting up
Explain that you are going to design and make cages for the pets. Think together about the requirements for individual pets.

What to do
Ask each child to choose which animal they will make a cage for. Tell them to think about the size and shape of box they will need. Ask if they like the box as it is or would they like to decorate it? Look at colour charts and let the children try to mix paint to create the colour they would like to use. Will it be comfortable as it is or does it need some form of bedding? What texture would be suitable? Do the individual pets need particular features for their cages? (A perch in a budgie's cage or a wheel for a hamster.) Try to develop the children's own imaginative ideas for creating these accessories, using as many different materials and resources as possible. Make the wire netting on the front of cages by fixing string to one side of the box, using the tapestry needle and weaving the ends in and out to the other side. Doors could be cut out of the cardboard and fixed with treasury tags. Bend and join pipe cleaners to make wheels and make a perch from a suitably shaped twig stuck in to modelling clay.

Questions to ask
How closely do the things we can use to make pretend cages represent the real thing? What is not the same? (The strength of the cage, perch, wheel.) How easy is it to make an exact circle or square?

For younger children
Ask these children to help you design an outside 'run' for pets recovering at the surgery. Encourage imaginative ideas and avoid too much adult input. Ideas could include wide-diameter cardboard tube runs, large building block mazes and cushion hills.

For older children
Pets arriving at the surgery will need smaller carrying cages. Can the children design these, perhaps using large shoe boxes. Wait for their ideas but, if they get stuck, you could suggest plaited string handles. How will the animals breathe?

Follow-up activities
• Ask the children to describe how they would feel when they saw their pets enjoying their specially created environment.
• During imaginative play in the surgery, use the cages they have made for carrying pets around and for use when the vet is looking after them.
• Examine simple shapes in the surgery, such as, squares and rectangles for cages, circles in food bowls and cylinders in feeding bottles.

CHAPTER FOUR

The colours and patterns found in a Flower Shop provide a rich source of stimulating learning material for young children. Follow the ideas on page 8 to set up a Flower Shop, and use these activities to explore shape and size in flowers, the conditions required for growing plants and to appreciate colour and texture when creating collage flowers.

PETALS

Learning objective
Language and Literacy – To give the children practise at writing their own names.

Group size
Up to eight children.

What you need
Several different shaped petals from real flowers. Thin card in bright colours, pencils, coloured pencils, erasers, paper fasteners, scissors and skewer (for adult use only).

Setting up
Cut large petal shapes (large enough for the children to write their own names on) from the thin card. Set up a table with these petal shapes and the other equipment.

What to do
Explain that you are going to make some flowers for the Flower Shop. Examine the flower petals noticing any special colour markings. Ask the children to write their name on a card petal shape and then to decorate the edges as they might be in a real flower, using the coloured pencils. Encourage them to write on as many card petals as possible, trying to improve the letter formation each time using upper and lower case letters correctly. Suggest that they could write each letter in a different colour. When you have enough petals to make a flower, make a hole in them all with a skewer. Fix the petals together with a brass paper fastener, fanning them out to make a flower.

Questions to ask
Why do we need a capital letter here? (Because it is at the beginning of a name.) Are you sitting comfortably? Are you holding your pencil in the right way? How do we begin this letter? Which way do we go now? Which letter do you have to write next?

For younger children
Help younger children by writing their names on to petals first. Ask them to find a petal with their own name and then to copy this on to another one. For those who still find it difficult to write their names independently, write the letters with dots so that the children can go over them.

For older children
Invite each child to make their own flower, using petals with their name and also petals with simple facts about themselves. For example; Emma, I am 5. I have blue eyes. I like dogs. Encourage the children to spell out simple words, but offer help when they are stuck, by writing short sentences for them to copy onto petals.

Follow-up activities
• Make an order book for the Flower Shop. Stick flower pictures in the book and let children decide which flowers they would like to give as a present by writing their names against the relevant picture.
• Write 'to' and 'from' labels for flower bouquets.
• Use a small amount of potting compost in a flat tray for tracing letter shapes.

ALL SHAPES AND SIZES

Learning objective
Mathematics – To examine shape, size and quantity.

Group size
Up to eight children.

What you need
A wide selection of flowers and leaves, together with some of the flowers you have made for the Flower Shop.

Setting up
Spread out the flowers and leaves on a large table. Ask the children to sit around the table and explain that they are going to look carefully at the different sizes and shapes in the flowers and leaves on the table in front of them.

What to do
Start by looking at a circular flower head, such as a chrysanthemum. Point out the shape to the children and name it as a circle. Look for the small circle shape inside the larger one. Explain that the outer circle is made up of individual petals. Their shape is different and is called oval. Look at how many petals make up the outer circle. Count the number of petals on other flowers. Notice that some have many more than others. This will also apply to the self-made flowers. Carefully examine other flowers and leaves and the markings on them, looking out for triangle and diamond shapes and noticing the cylinder shape of the stems. Look out for spheres such as those on dandelion seed heads. Encourage the children to tell you what irregularly shaped flowers and leaves remind them of. Look carefully at the different sizes of leaves and petals.

Questions to ask
Which flower has the most petals? Can you find the biggest leaf? What shapes can you see in this flower? Can you find the thinnest stem? Can you find a wide and a narrow-triangle-shaped leaf? How many thorns are on this rose? (CARE!)

For younger children
Restrict the number of flowers and leaves and use ones with distinctive shapes. Choose flowers without too many petals.

For older children
Sort flowers and leaves according to shape and size. Make a line of leaves going from the thinnest to the fattest. Line up the flower heads so that the one with least petals is first and the one with the most petals is last.

Follow-up activities
• Make some pot plants using suitably shaped twigs. Stick these in modelling clay in flower pots and help the children to cut out some of the leaf shapes they have seen to stick on to the twigs.
• Attach large leaves to the table with a small piece of adhesive tape and fix a sheet of paper over the top. Make leaf rubbings, using wax crayons on their sides.
• Take a walk outside. Find the tallest tree. Find the smallest flower. How many flowers in the flower-bed/tub?

COMPARING NOTES

Learning objective
Personal and Social Development – To develop an ability to establish effective relationships with adults.

Group size
Up to eight children.

What you need
Several willing, green-fingered parents who will come in to the group to spend some time talking to the children.

Setting up
Explain to the parent volunteers that you are trying to encourage the children to listen to adults speaking about their interests and also to encourage children to ask questions to develop their knowledge and understanding. Ask parents to try to keep their explanations as simple as they can and if possible to bring in examples of some of the things they have grown. Sit the children in a circle on the floor and explain that a visitor is coming in to talk to them about their own garden and what grows in it.

What to do
Begin by introducing the parent and welcoming them. Explain that the visitor is going to speak first while the children listen and then it will be their turn to ask any questions they would like to by putting their hands up and waiting for their turn. Take a back-seat and allow your visitor to take 'centre-stage'.

Questions to ask
What are all the things we might find in a garden? Does your garden have a – wall, tree, flower-bed, path, hedge, pond? If you don't have a garden, do you visit a park near your home? Do you know the names of any flowers or trees that grow in your garden or the park? How do carrots, strawberries, apples and so on grow? Why do we grow things in gardens and parks? (Because they are colourful to look at, they can have beautiful scents are good for wildlife and may be grown for selling in flower shops.)

For younger children
Reverse the procedure for discussion by asking the children to talk about their experiences of gardens (their own or ones they have visited) first. Encourage the parent to extend this discussion by bringing in facts about their own.

For older children
Ask parents to share their interest and enthusiasm for gardening by involving the children in planting and looking after some flowers (indoor or outdoor) for the group.

Follow-up activities
• If your visitors can spare some flowers from their gardens, help the children to make these into posies for selling in the shop.
• Provide a small, shallow tray and a selection of small stones, moss, twigs and flowers for each child to make into a miniature garden. Display these in a corner of the flower shop.
• Recite the rhyme 'Mary, Mary, quite contrary' and create a wall display of all the things that grow in her garden.

HOW DO FLOWERS GROW?

Learning objective
Knowledge and
Understanding of the
World – To learn about
how plants grow.

Group size
Up to six children.

What you need
Several small plastic flower pots, potting compost, watering can, quick growing seeds (such as sunflowers or corn), adhesive labels, black sugar paper, felt-tipped pen.

Setting up
Label the pots: water, warm, light; no water, warm, light; water, cold, light; water, warm, dark; water, cold, dark. Bear in mind that seeds need water, warm conditions and light to grow into strong healthy plants.

What to do
Half-fill each pot with compost, put in a few seeds and cover with more compost. Treat the seeds, according to the instructions on the labels. Find safe places to store them – either in the warmth of the flower shop, on a shelf in a fridge or on a cold windowsill. Cover with a black paper cone to keep out the light. Make sure that the children examine the pots every day and, if the seeds are supposed to be kept damp, that they are watered sparingly. If all goes according to plan, all the pots which have been watered should be showing some signs of growth within a few days. Those which have been deprived of warmth should be noticeably smaller than the others and shoots which have been growing in the dark should be distinctly yellow. The strongest and healthiest looking growth should have occurred in the pot which has been watered, kept warm and given plenty of light.

Questions to ask
What do these shoots look like in comparison to those? How long did they take to grow? Why do you think they are yellow instead of green? What do your seeds need that they haven't had?

For younger children
Restrict the number of variables to: water, light and warmth; no water, light and warmth; water, dark and warmth. Work with a group of four children.

For older children
Try growing flower seeds on sand or cotton wool as compost. Compare the results, to show the need for a rich growing medium.

Follow-up activities
• Sell the resulting plants from this activity in the Flower Shop. Make labels giving directions for looking after the plants. The children could draw symbols for water (drops), warmth (sun) and light (a light bulb).
• Pull up a growing shoot and look carefully at the roots as well as the shoot. Notice how the seed has split open, the shoot has grown up and the roots down.
• Stand white-coloured daffodils in water, coloured with food dye for a few days. You will soon notice that the flower has coloured tips to its petals. This is a good way of proving that flowers 'drink' water.

SUNFLOWERS

Learning objective
Physical Development – To handle small tools, objects and modelling materials with increasing control.

Group size
Up to eight children.

What you need
A real or artificial sunflower or a large picture of one, clay, blunt knives or modelling tools, poster paint, brushes, PVA adhesive, small brown collage pieces, pots and palettes, plastic table covering, aprons.

Setting up
Cover the table with plastic covering and give each child an apron to wear. Put modelling tools in the middle of the table. Look carefully at the sunflower you have available, noticing petal shape and colour in particular. Explain that they are all going to make one big sunflower.

What to do
Give each child a lump of self-hardening clay. Ask them to split this lump in half and to use each piece to make one petal for the big sunflower. Allow them to use blunt knives or modelling tools if necessary, to achieve the shape they want. (CARE!) Roll another lump of clay into a ball and put it flat to make a thick circle. As each child completes a petal, help him/her to fix it onto your circle, that will make the flower centre, by smoothing the edges together so that they fuse. Fix the first eight petals round the circle and the next eight, in between the first so that an overlapping effect is produced. When the sunflower head is complete, let it dry out completely. Next, let each child paint some of it, mixing their own shades of yellow and brown. When dry again, return to the centre of the flower and use PVA adhesive to stick on a variety of small brown collage materials (CARE!), such as lentils, currants, gravel, sunflower seeds and thick wool. When this is all dry, ask the children to coat the whole flower with PVA adhesive in order to create a varnished effect. Display the completed, giant sunflower outside the florist shop.

Questions to ask
How can you make the clay smooth, flat or bend? How can you make sure that this knife doesn't hurt anyone? How can you stick the bits on firmly?

For younger children
Let each child make their own small sunflower, making petal shapes from one ball of clay. Complete as above.

For older children
Having worked with clay, encourage the children to try other modelling materials, such as Plasticine or various forms of play dough. Which is the easiest to work with to give the desired results?

Follow-up activities
• Try making flowers out of coloured marzipan. Roll out the marzipan and cut out leaves and petals, using a blunt knife or shape-cutters. Squeeze petals together to form flowers. Offer them to customers in the shop.
• Using various sizes of paintbrushes, foam brushes, rollers, sponges and poster paint, create flowers to decorate the outside of the Flower Shop.
• Using small construction kits or mosaic shapes, try making flower shapes.

BEAUTIFUL FLOWERS

Learning objective
Creative Development – To explore and appreciate colour and texture.

Group size
Up to six children.

What you need
Several different fabric remnants, scissors, PVA adhesive, brushes, sorting trays, card in different colours, adhesive tape, small garden canes, large plastic flower pots, modelling clay, photocopiable page 62.

Setting up
Examine pictures of a range of flowers, including exotic ones from hot countries. Provide each child with a sorting tray, a pot of PVA adhesive and a paint brush. Cut out flower shapes in card, using the photocopiable templates on page 62.

What to do
Ask the children to choose a flower shape. Explain that you are going to make flowers by sticking small pieces of fabric onto the flower shapes, choosing shades that will match the colour of the card. Ask the children to select fabric from the remnants. Encourage them to look carefully for colours within patterns and to look for all shades of their colour, for example a flower which will be yellow could also have pale orange, gold, cream and fawn in it. Help them to cut their fabric into small pieces, allowing the children to practise their own cutting skills on the easier materials such as felt. Stick pieces on to the flower template, alternating shades and patterns as much as possible. When dry, trim the edges of the card, mount the flowers on to small garden canes using adhesive tape and display in the Flower Shop by sticking the canes into large plastic flower pots half-filled with modelling clay.

Questions to ask
What does this fabric feel like? How many different colours and shades can you see? Which is the darkest/lightest? Which colours look good together?

For younger children
Restrict the fabric for sorting, removing too many patterned pieces. Cut the fabric into larger pieces, for easier handling and to cover flower templates more quickly.

For older children
Ask the children to select fabric using two criteria for sorting such as colour and texture, rather than just colour. Explain that they are going to make silky, red flowers or thick, purple ones.

Follow-up activities
• Take a walk outside and let the children touch different textures – grass, gravel, goose grass, conker shells – and ask them to describe what they feel like. Take great care not to let them touch anything poisonous and wash hands carefully afterwards.
• Let the children investigate the colours made by mixing small amounts of powder paint in a palette. How do they make lighter and darker shades?
• Put several samples of fabric, (velvet, silk, lace, cotton, corduroy and tweed), into a pillow case. By putting their hands inside, can the children identify them by touch alone?

CHAPTER FIVE

Use children's natural enthusiasm for the seaside and set up a Seaside Café, as described on page 8, to make an exciting play environment. Using their knowledge of food and drink, they can practise skills of one-to-one correspondence when laying the table, observe changes which take place during cooking and use different techniques to create a seaside collage.

CAROLINE'S CAFÉ

Learning objective
Language and Literacy – To develop an understanding of the phonic sounds of letters.

Group size
Whole group.

What you need
Plenty of ideas for names of cafés and food beginning with the same letter sound. Prepare these well in advance so that you keep ideas flowing easily.

Setting up
Sit the children around you in a circle and talk about cafés and restaurants that they may have been to. Talk about the names of these and the kinds of food they may have had there.

What to do
Ask each child in turn to think of some food to sell in their café which starts with the same letter sound as their own name. Try and make connections with the seaside. For example, Clare could sell crab sandwiches, Mary – mussels, Freddie – fish, Sanjay – samosas, Vanessa – vegetables, Peter – pasta, Nancy – noodles and so on.

Extend the activity by asking the children to think of a welcoming sign for their café, for example, 'Fatima's Food', 'Simon's Snacks' or 'Lucy's Lunches'. If the child's name does not begin with the usual phonic sound for that letter, associate it with a similar sound. For example, 'Sian's shop' and 'Georgina sells jelly'. Put up new shop signs every few days.

Questions to ask
Can you hear the sound that starts you name? Can you think of a word which starts with the same sound? Can you hear the same sound in these two words?

For younger children
Try to keep the foods very simple – food with which the children are familiar. Bear in mind that your seaside café could sell other things as well as food, for example, 'Pablo's Place' could have paddles as well as prawns!

For older children
Encourage the children to make a complete list of things beginning with the same phonic sound as their name, to sell in the shop.

Follow-up activities
• Practise identifying the rhyming words in rhymes such as; Sam has jam and ham; Tess makes less mess; Joffy has coffee and toffee and Pete can eat meat.
• Think of foods beginning with some phonic blends and digraphs, for example, br...bread, ch...chapatis and sp...spaghetti.
• Write menus: encourage the children to sound out some of the simple words they want to use but offer help where necessary.

TABLE FOR FOUR

Learning objective
Mathematics – To practise counting and matching, using everyday objects.

Group size
Up to four children.

What you need
Table-cloths, mats, knives, forks and spoons, glasses, small flower arrangements, menus.

Setting up
If possible, take your whole group on an outing to a local café. Explain that the children are now going to set up their own café and to work as waiters and waitresses.

What to do
Let two children be responsible for one table. Ask them to arrange it and lay it for a specific number of people – either three or four. Encourage the children to count out loud as they select plates and cutlery to reinforce the numbers and the necessity for one knife for one place and so on. Offer help if required but they should be able to do this independently. Once the table is laid out correctly, encourage other children from your group to come in to the café as customers. Let your waiters take orders from their table's customers. Use pretend food and drink, produced from another corner of your room. Encourage accurate counting, matching objects one-to-one as the children prepare orders. You could introduce a colour theme for each table, matching cloths, mats, cutlery, menus and flowers.

Questions to ask
How many people are going to eat here? So, how many mats, knives, forks and so on will we need to put on the table? How will we fit four people around this table? How many chairs will we need? Is there room for anyone else?

For younger children
Lay tables for one or two people, keeping the counting and matching very simple.

For older children
How many ways can two tables be laid for seven people? Can they have one for three and one for four; one for five and one for two; one for six and one for one? Can they push two tables together to make room for seven people?

Follow-up activities
• Practise recognising and writing numbers up to ten. Can the children count out ten sweets to put into a bowl to offer to their customers as they leave the café?
• Can the children work out how many more plates and so on they will need if an extra person comes to their table? Can they work out three and one and four and one orally?

GOOD BEHAVIOUR!

Learning objective
Personal and Social Development – To develop good manners, a sense of responsibility and independence in dressing and personal hygiene.

Group size
Whole group.

What you need
A time when the children are getting ready for a meal or their mid-morning drink and a time when they are getting ready to go outside to play.

Setting up
Talk to the children about the importance of good manners, socially acceptable behaviour and careful personal hygiene. Set the scene for a role-play situation. When they are going out to play, pretend they are going to the café. When they are eating or drinking, pretend they are in the café and when they come in from play, pretend they are back at home.

What to do
Before the children go outside, allow plenty of time for them to try to put on and do up their own coats. When they come in again, make sure they hang everything up themselves. Before meals, make sure children wash their hands carefully and during meals or drinks time, let the children know that you are watching them carefully and that you are expecting good manners. Ask the children to make their own lists of do's and don'ts, for example: do sit still and do not speak with your mouth full. When the children are handed food or drinks or they choose their own, make sure they say please and thank you. Reinforce acceptable behaviour further when the children line up by emphasising that you expect them to stand quietly and not to push anyone.

Questions to ask
Why do we need to have good manners? What will people feel like if we push them? Why do you need to learn how to do up your own coat? Why must we wash hands before meals? Why should you hang up your own coat tidily? Why must we ask for things nicely and thank people when we get what we want?

For younger children
Offer younger children more help and concentrate on one particular area of development at a time, such as, putting possessions away tidily when they have finished with them.

For older children
Explore together a set of rules for your group. What do the children feel they could do to improve the quality of the group as a whole?

Follow-up activities
• Pretend it is a very snowy day when you are going out for a meal. Practise changing boots for shoes as you enter the café.
• At meal times, practise holding knives and forks correctly and cutting up food.
• Talk together about how we keep the different parts of our bodies clean and healthy – teeth, hair, hands, nails and so on. Use the photocopiable sheet on page 63 for reinforcement.

FEELING HUNGRY?

Learning objective
Knowledge and Understanding of the World – To observe changes which take place during cooking.

Group size
Up to six children.

What you need
Ideally, a separate room where the children can watch from a safe distance, as you use a cooker. Failing this, a small electric ring and a toaster. (CARE!) You will also need white sliced bread, eggs, potatoes, a frying pan or wok, saucepans, spoon, knife, fish slice, potato masher, wooden spoon and potato peeler, oil and butter.

Setting up
Talk to the children about safety in the kitchen. Make sure they understand the need to sit still and watch as you cook. Make it clear that they will all see what has happened to the food and that you want them to tell you how it has changed.

What to do
Let the children examine a slice of white bread. Tell them to note the texture, smell and taste as well as its appearance. Toast two slices – one lightly and the other, so that it is on the point of burning. Examine the results once the toast has cooled down.

Next, let one of the children (CARE! – beware of allergies to eggs) crack an egg into a dish, taking care not to break the yolk. Ask them to describe the raw white and yolk. Boil another egg for about six minutes. Once it has cooled, allow another child to peel it and then cut it in half, lengthways.

Peel a few potatoes and chop them up. Let each child have a small piece to examine, noting especially how hard the potato is. Boil some potatoes for about ten minutes and let the children mash them noting how easy this is now that the potato is cooked.

Questions to ask
Has the food changed? How? Does it feel, look, smell and taste different? What has caused it to change? Can you change it back to its original state?

For younger children
Make jelly. Look carefully at the raw cubes, and then notice how they dissolve in warm water and how the jelly solidifies again when it cools.

For older children
Use some more eggs and examine the changes which take place after frying and scrambling.

Follow-up activities
• Cook some chocolate crispies to use in the café. Point out how the chocolate changes as it is heated up and how it becomes hard again as it cools.
• During role-play in the café, sample various fruit and vegetables in their raw state. Now cook them and note how they change.
• Hold a group session, trying to guess how other food, for example pasta, cheese and rice, will change when it is cooked.

HAVE FUN!

Learning objective
Physical Development – To handle tools safely when manipulating wet sand.

Group size
Up to eight children, depending on the size of your sandpit.

What you need
A sandpit filled with wet sand, spades, other digging and burrowing tools, rakes, moulds and buckets.

Setting up
Talk to the children about the need for great care when playing with sand, to avoid sand particles going into people's eyes. Explain that you want the children to experiment with the wet sand, imagining it to be the beach close to the Seaside Café. Give them various tools and equipment to see whether they can create the shapes and effects they want. Remind them that their own hands may well be the most effective tools of all.

What to do
Ask the children to spread out along the sides of the sandpit so that they all have plenty of room to play with the tools and to make their own constructions. Watch as they handle the tools and help them to use these more effectively if this is appropriate. Emphasise the need for greater care when they are using heavy, long-handled or sharp tools so that no-one else is hurt by them. Allow the children plenty of time for independent free exploration. Then encourage them to co-operate as a whole group, to try to make a joint castle or construction of their own choosing.

Follow-up activities
• Consider taking your group to the seaside for an outing (CARE!). Build a giant sand-castle on the beach. Invite all the children to help with digging and patting the sand together. Visit a real Seaside Café.
• Compare the results of building in dry, wet and very wet sand. Which gives the best result and which is the easiest sand to manipulate?
• Talk about safety on the beach; for example, the current which could carry people out of their depth and sharp rocks and shells which can cut bare feet.

Questions to ask
How can we make a tower? How can we make sure it does not fall down? How can we make a tunnel through this pile of sand? Which tool should I use here?

For younger children
Ask the children to make sand-castles using only small buckets and spades. Encourage them to repeat the exercise several times to see what they can do to make the resulting castle more perfect.

For older children
Experiment to see how tall a tower or how long a tunnel they can make. Which are the most effective tools to use – their hands or buckets and spades?

BY THE SEASIDE

Learning objective
*Creative Development
– To explore ways of
representing seaside
life in a collage.*

Group size
Up to eight children.

What you need

Pictures of the seaside and sea life. Card, thin paper, PVA adhesive, small collage pieces (CARE!), including sequins, fabric, shiny paper, tissue paper and ribbons. Natural sponge, poster paint, brushes, palettes, twigs and pipe cleaners, needles and thread, plastic food bag, bubble wrap.

Setting up

Look at several seaside pictures with the children and examine the shapes, colours and textures of different kinds of fish, other sea creatures and seaweed. Explain that they are going to make a collage to decorate the café.

What to do

Start by drawing some fish on to card. Let the children paint these, mixing their own paints to produce realistic colours. Encourage them to choose collage materials or shiny paper to add scales and specific markings. Use textured fabric or paper to create crab shells and twigs or pipe cleaners for the legs. An octopus can be added using different shades of paint sponged on to a card outline. Make 'seaweed' out of textured and frayed fabric, tissue paper and thin ribbon. Cut out some shell shapes in pastel card and sew patterns on these shapes, first piercing the card with a needle in suitable places. Make a jelly fish from an inflated plastic food bag (CARE!) and strips of bubble wrap. Assemble the collage on the walls of the café.

Questions to ask

Have you see any of these sea creatures? How can we make ours look like these? Can you find anything in these oddments which we could use for fish eyes, crab claws and so on? What does this piece of wood/paper/material/plastic remind you of?

For younger children

Draw buckets, spades, boats and balls as well as sea creatures. Encourage the children to paint these in bright colours.

For older children

Float tiny amounts of marbling ink on water in a shallow tray. Carefully place thin paper on to the surface of the water, to absorb the ink pattern. Use these designs to cut up and use on fish shapes.

Follow-up activities
• Create bubbles for the fish by putting a mixture of paint and washing up liquid in a yoghurt pot. Blow gently (CARE!) through a straw into the mixture until the bubbles froth up. Carefully press a thin piece of paper down on to the pot, remove it gently to find a bubble pattern on the paper.
• Draw an outline of a mermaid. Let the children paint and decorate her.
• Use coloured card cut into different shapes, to create sailing boats.
• Make some 'sand-castles' by drawing the shapes in glue, onto card, scattering dry sand over the top and shaking off any excess.

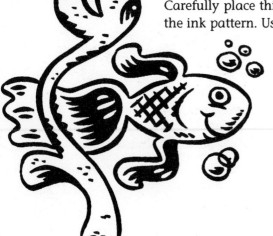

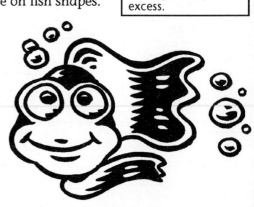

Set up a Post Office using the ideas on page 9 to provide a wealth of role-play opportunities. With this theme children can explore ways of wrapping parcels, giving them practise in the skills of estimating and practical problem solving as well as experiencing designing and making cards for different purposes. Children will love sorting through and sending authentic parcels and letters!

FUNNY STORIES

Learning objective
Language and Literacy – To encourage children to make up stories and to express their thoughts with increasing fluency.

Group size
Up to eight children.

What you need
A selection of postcards, especially showing animals, people and forms of transport.

Setting up
Sit in a circle with the children and explain that you are going to make up a story altogether, based on the pictures in some of the postcards which are for sale in the Post Office.

What to do
Let the children select four postcards, making sure that they select some with animals or people and some with locations or transport. In order to build confidence and spark ideas, begin the first story yourself. Having selected postcards with a rabbit, a monkey, an aeroplane and a tropical island, you could start: 'Once upon a time, there was a little rabbit called Reginald. He had a friend called Millie, the monkey. They were both very fond of flying.' Ask for volunteers to continue the story, making sure that all the children join in and have a turn. Encourage any ideas. It does not matter how strange or unlikely the story becomes, but try to keep it going for a reasonable length of time. When it is clear that the children are losing interest or have run out of ideas, tactfully draw this story to a satisfactory conclusion and begin the process again with a new set of postcards.

Questions to ask
What happens next? Is this part of the story happy/sad/exciting/frightening? How would you feel if you were having this adventure? How would you like the story to end?

For younger children
Give more direction to younger children. Encourage them to develop your basic ideas. For instance, if the story takes the characters to a shop, what kind of shop was it and what did they buy?

For older children
Introduce more rules into the story telling. Can someone make the story exciting/make something funny happen/describe the weather?

Follow-up activities
• Ask the children to imagine that the postman brings them a letter or parcel. Can they describe how they feel when they get this?
• Use postcards in the Post Office, to encourage the use of adjectives. If there is a beach scene ask: what sort of beach is it, what are people wearing, what is the weather like?
• Read the children a story and ask them to retell it in their own words. Ask them to identify different parts of the story which are happy/sad/exciting/funny/frightening.

IS THERE ANY POST?

Learning objective
Mathematics – To practise estimating and solving practical problems.

Group size
Up to four children.

What you need
Empty boxes, cartons, plastic bottles and cardboard tubes of all shapes and sizes, including spheres, thin brown wrapping paper, adhesive tape, scissors, string, used stamps, pencils, card, PVA adhesive.

Setting up
Spread out all the boxes, together with large sheets of wrapping paper. Explain that you will be asking the children to help you to wrap up the cartons and boxes to look like parcels, for posting in the Post Office. Encourage them to look carefully at the shape and size of the boxes and think about how to cover them neatly.

What to do
Ask each child to choose something to wrap. Ask them to estimate how much paper they will need and then to cut off what they think will be enough. Offer help where necessary as the children try to wrap their parcels. If the amount of paper is clearly not enough or much too much, encourage the child to think again. You may find it helpful to suggest that they place the item on the paper and wrap it very roughly before they cut off their piece of paper.

Once the item is fully covered, help to fix the paper with adhesive tape. Next, think about how much string will be needed to tie around the parcel. Again, ask the children to estimate and to cut off what they require. Help them to tie knots or bows. If they have not cut off enough string, help them to think again. Complete the parcels by attaching stamps according to the length of the parcel: ask the children to draw around their hand onto card and cut it out as a measure. Add one stamp to the parcel for each 'hand-span' of length.

Questions to ask
Which is the best way to wrap this present? Shall we turn it this way or that way? Which is the longest parcel? Which parcel do you think will need the most stamps?

For younger children
Instead of using paper, can the children choose slightly bigger boxes to wrap the small boxes and cartons in? Make sure they choose ones which will close comfortably with their item inside.

For older children
Can these children think of an easier way to wrap an awkward shape, such as a ball? Will this require more or less paper?

Follow-up activities
• Let the children guess which size envelope is required for several shapes and sizes of greetings cards.
• Practise folding letters so that they fit neatly into different envelopes.
• Ask the children to guess whether they will be able to post certain items through the letter-box. Having guessed, let them try.

HEY, MR POSTMAN!

Learning objective
Personal and Social Development – To practise taking turns and sharing.

Group size
Up to five children.

What you need
The Post Office set up as described on page 9.

Setting up
Point out the need to share and take turns as you encourage children to take on different roles while playing in the Post Office.

What to do
Outline the different roles that the children can adopt and encourage them to decide between themselves who will take which role initially. The postman will need a hat and bag for letters and parcels and can unload the post box and deliver letters to the other children. The person serving at the Post Office counter will need to weigh parcels, give out stamps, money for allowances, postal orders, television licences and so on. The Post Office shop assistant will be responsible for selling items such as cards, wrapping paper, padded envelopes, tape and string. Customers can come in with any requests or requirements or just to post letters and parcels. Watch the children carefully and aim for co-operative play, with everyone enjoying themselves and taking a full, constructive part. Join in – in any role – to move the play in new directions or to avoid potential conflicts by creating other interests.

Questions to ask
(In role) What sort of card would you like? Who is it for? What size of envelope do you need? When is the post collected? Do you need these letters to get to people quickly? Can you help me to fill in this form?

For younger children
Give the children a definite assignment for their role-play. For example, 'go and post these letters'; 'buy a stamp for this parcel'; 'buy a card for Grandma's birthday'; 'deliver these parcels to the rest of the group'.

For older children
When the children have played in the Post Office for a while, assess together whether it is arranged in the best way to give everyone enough space to fulfil their roles successfully. Make any alterations necessary.

Follow-up activities
• At the end of the role-play session, encourage group co-operation by making sure that everything is put back where it belongs.
• Encourage children to bring in collections of stamps or any first-day cover envelopes. Give each child a chance to examine these carefully.
• Choose a different child each day to be the 'group postman', giving out any letters/pictures which need to go home to parents.
• Discuss together why it is right to share and take turns and wrong to keep everything for ourselves and to always demand attention.

HOME SWEET HOME

Learning objective
Knowledge and Understanding of the World – To encourage children to talk about where they live, their families and events in their own lives.

Group size
Up to eight children.

What you need
Postcards of the cities/towns/villages in which your children live, local newspapers (both of which are on sale in the Post Office) letters and cards written to the children from members of their families celebrating special events in their lives, old greetings cards.

Setting up
Sit at the table and have all these things available. Explain that you would like the children to tell you all about where they live, their families and what has already happened in their lives.

What to do
Start by looking at the postcards of local cities, towns and villages. Can the children identify where they live? Can they recognise anything in the postcard and tell you about it? If there is anything particularly unusual do they know what it is? Next, let each child in turn show others in the group some letters and cards they have received from family members. Ask them to tell you who they are from and how that person fits into their family. Have an open discussion about events in the children's lives, asking some of the questions outlined below.

Questions to ask
What sort of houses can you see? Are there any shops? Is there a church? Can you see a river/a pond/a park/a very tall building/a statue? Are there lots of people? How are people travelling around? Why did you get this card? What can you remember about the event? What has changed in your life since then? How have you changed?

For younger children
Ask each child to draw or paint a picture of their house. Mount this on card with a pocket underneath in which they can keep their cards and letters from family members. Encourage each child to talk about where they live (their picture), their family and their birthdays (from the letters and cards).

For older children
In the local newspapers, search for interesting pictures of places the children might be able to identify. Look also for pictures of events they might know about. Encourage all the children to tell you as much as possible about the pictures.

Follow-up activities
• Set up a mini sorting office. Write each child's name on a separate shoe box. Ask all the children to write their names on three old greetings cards. Mix these up on a table and let each child have a turn at matching the cards to the correct boxes.
• Look at all the postcards in the Post Office. How can the children tell whether they have come from this country? Look at stamps from other areas of the world.
• Ask each child to draw a picture of all the members of his/her family.
• Write a group book about 'The best thing in my life so far'.

HAPPY BIRTHDAY

Learning objective
Physical Development – To practise handling tools and objects with increasing control and to improve manipulative skills.

Group size
Up to eight children.

What you need
Pieces of A5 card, white newsprint paper, poster paints, flat trays, items for printing (biscuit cutters, LEGO bricks, potato mashers, small wooden bricks, jar lids, natural sponge, dowelling), sequins, PVA adhesive, pencils, thin brushes, plastic table covering, two tables.

Setting up
Cover the tables with plastic covering. Mix poster paint in various colours to a fairly runny consistency and pour a thin layer into each flat tray. Put the items for printing in the middle of this table and two large sheets of newsprint at each side. On the other table, put out the sequins in flat trays, four very small amounts of PVA adhesive in shallow lids and four pieces of A5 card, folded in half.

What to do
Explain that they are going to make wrapping paper and 'age' birthday cards to sell in the Post Office. Set up the wrapping paper table first. Let the children choose items to print with and the colours they wish to use. Dip the items in the paint, wiping off any excess and press them carefully onto the paper in the chosen positions. Ask the children to work in pairs. Encourage them to cover the whole of their paper.

Set up the birthday card table. Let each child choose which age their card will be for. Lightly draw a large number in pencil on their card. Let them apply adhesive over this figure with a thin brush. Show each child how to cover their number carefully with sequins. Dip the very tip of a pencil into the adhesive and pick up one sequin with this. Put it carefully in position on the number. Repeat with the next sequins until the whole number is covered. This requires careful concentration but many children will become fully absorbed in the activity.

Questions to ask
Are you getting a good print? Is your paint too runny/too thick? Why do we need to use only a very small amount of adhesive?

For younger children
Use the larger items for printing the paper with younger children. Let them pick up sequins in their fingers, and place them carefully on the number, one at a time.

For older children
Try taping two or three pencils together to use for printing spotty wrapping paper. Encourage the children to come up with their own ideas for objects to use for printing.

Follow-up activities
• Try weaving paper. Take a sheet of A5 card, fold it in half and make deep cuts from the folded edge, stopping before you reach the other edge. Open out and weave thin strips of paper in and out of the card strips.
• Practise sewing on squares of Binca.

GUESS WHAT?

Learning objective
Creative Development
– To explore shape and
form in three
dimensions and to
develop the senses of
touch, hearing and
smell.

Group size
Whole group.

What you need
Several parcels which you have carefully wrapped in thin brown paper for use in the Post Office. You will need enough for each child to have one – some with a fairly strong smell (soap, a packet of coffee, a lemon), some which make a noise when you shake them (a bell, a rattle) and some which are only recognised by careful touching (a hairbrush, a buttoned cardigan). You will also need a few extra ones which can be easily recognised by shape only (ball, triangle, book, large building brick).

Setting up
Sit everyone down in a big circle and introduce the game. You will be asking the children to use all their senses to try to work out what is in the parcels, without opening them. Do they remember the excitement of trying to guess what is in stockings at Christmas, in presents on St. Nicholas' Day or in gifts given at Diwali, Hanukkah and Chinese New Year (Yuan Tan)?

What to do
Start by holding up each 'shape' parcel in turn to see if the children can guess what it is just by looking at it. Choose a different child to answer each time. Having explored answers from everyone, identify the most popular answer and then ask one child to open the parcel to check their guesses. Next give each child a separate parcel to work with. Encourage them to use all their senses (except taste!) to try to find out what is inside, again without opening the parcel. Allow exploration for a reasonable length of time and then ask them to swap parcels with their neighbour. Repeat the exploration. When both children are satisfied that they know what is inside their parcels, let them open them to check.

Questions to ask
What shape is your parcel? Does it make a noise/smell? What does it feel like? What do you think it could be? Were you right?

For younger children
Concentrate on the two senses of looking and feeling. Use items which provide a mixture of interesting shapes and textures.

For older children
Extend the activity by including several different instruments in the parcels. Can the children identify them by sound only?

Follow-up activities
• Examine the parcels in the Post Office. Can the children sort them by size, thickness, length and three dimensional shape?
• Can the children fit all the parcels into a small sack or onto a single shelf? How do they have to arrange them to take up the minimum space?
• Play a 'guess the material' game. Use a simple blindfold and hand the children different objects made from plastic, wood, fabric and metal.

CHAPTER SEVEN

A quiet area of the room designated as a Library, that is lovingly cared for and created by the children will encourage them to respect and treasure books. Set the scene using the ideas on page 9 to provide a context for teaching early literacy skills in a fun way. Children can also learn how to use cassette recorders and how to design and make their own story books.

BOOKS, BOOKS, GLORIOUS BOOKS!

Learning objective
Language and Literacy – To enjoy books and to understand that words and pictures carry meaning.

Group size
Up to eight children.

What you need
A wide selection of books – stories, poetry, information books, picture books, 'Big books' and, if possible, books the children have made themselves, display stands and book boxes, comfortable chairs and cushions, peace and quiet!

Setting up
Make sure that your Library is cosy and comfortable and that books are easily accessible and attractively displayed.

What to do
Make sure that the children understand the need for quiet in a library, remembering visits they may have had to a real library. Encourage them to handle all the books freely and to enjoy both individual and shared reading. End the session by reading a selection of different books to the children, making sure that they can all see clearly. Point to the print and the pictures as you read, to reinforce that words and pictures carry meaning.

Questions to ask
What kind of books do you like? Why? How does this book make you feel? How do we know what this book is about? (From the cover.) Can you read this story? If you get stuck on a word, how can we try to work it out? (From both the individual letters in the word, from the context of all the words and from the pictures in the story.)

For younger children
Try to have two adults in your Library, for individual attention. Have plenty of picture books, with no words, so that the children can tell the stories. Read a story with plenty of repeated words so that the children can join in.

For older children
Include more reference books, including encyclopaedias and atlases. Have fun finding out – where can we learn more about camels/our bones/drawing/China?

Follow-up activities
• Visit a local library and explore the children's section.
• Invite an author/ illustrator in to talk to the children.
• Write a group story. Base it on the children's ideas.
• Tell a simple story about familiar characters from films, nursery rhymes or popular books, using picture flash cards for as many of your words as possible. Encourage the children to join in as they recognise the pictures.

WHERE CAN I FIND IT?

Learning objective
Mathematics – To develop a familiarity with numbers up to ten and an awareness of number order.

Group size
Up to four children.

What you need
An interesting selection of information books and story books with more than one story. Make sure that all have clear numbers on each page and contents pages.

Setting up
Sit the children down at a table with a selection of books. Explain that they are going to explore what they can find out from the numbers in a book.

What to do
Remind the children about the formation of numbers one to ten. Can they count up to ten? Discuss how we hold a book in order to start reading it. Where is the beginning? Where is the end? Which way do we turn the pages? Then relate this to number order. Show them that we start counting at number one and the numbers get bigger and it is the same with page numbers. Point out that as the story develops from the beginning to the end, the page number gradually gets bigger. Ask the children to choose a short book and to open it at the beginning. What is the number on that page? Turn the pages, counting out loud as that number increases by one each time. Help the children to find the contents page at the front

of a book. Explain that this page is to tell you where to find a certain story or few pages about a particular thing (a chapter). Point to one of the numbers on this page. If necessary, help the children to name this number, to identify where it comes in the number sequence and therefore to say whether they expect to find it near the beginning or the end of the book.

Questions to ask
Why do we have numbers in a book? Have you seen this number before? Can you tell me what it is? What number comes after five? What number comes before nine?

For younger children
Concentrate on the number sequence to five, noting numbers on the pages of a relatively short book.

For older children
Help the children to read what is written opposite a chosen number on the contents page. Look together for this number to see whether you find what you expect on this page.

Follow-up activities
• Practise using an index in a children's encyclopaedia.
• Practise reciting number sequences up to ten with the children, beginning with a different number each time.
• Make number lines. Draw a snake with separate segments on the body. Let the children colour these in and then ink in some numbers in sequence.
• Can the children tell you the answers to simple 'add one' sums? In other words, what is the next number in the sequence?

ARE YOU SITTING COMFORTABLY?

Learning objective
Personal and Social Development – To enjoy books quietly and independently, asking adults for help as and when necessary.

Group size
Whole group.

What you need
The Library setting and peace and quiet!

Setting up
Make sure all the children have plenty of space and are sitting comfortably, within easy reach of a range of books.

What to do
Explain how a real library works and what kind of behaviour is expected when you visit a library. Make it clear that you expect a period of quiet reading with children looking at books on their own or in pairs, without disturbing the others. Make it part of the 'rules' that children should ask for help, if they need it, by putting up their hands and asking an adult quietly. Encourage perseverance in trying to work out the meaning of words or indeed what certain words say. Let the children choose their books, regardless of content or standard, thus encouraging new learning. Make sure that books are returned neatly to the shelves when children have finished looking at them.

Questions to ask
What sort of books do you like? What is this book about? If you can't read all the words, will it matter? What can you learn from the pictures? Where do you think you will find a book of poems?

For younger children
Restrict your book selection to simple picture story books and books without words. Include alphabet, shape, colour and counting books. Categorise books into areas, using plastic farm animals to show the location of books about animals, plastic letters to show where alphabet books will be and so on.

For older children
Pair up children so that you have a good reader together with a weaker one. Encourage both to read quietly to each other, letting the competent reader take on the role of the adult in providing help.

Follow-up activities
• Set a definite task such as finding out about different materials from books in the Library and ask the children to bring you evidence that they have completed that task.
• Help the children to increase their confidence by reading some of their book to the whole group, asking for help if necessary.
• Hold a tidying up session in the Library, mend any damaged books and stress the importance of looking after the Library environment and treating books carefully so that everyone can enjoy them.

ON, OFF, PAUSE!

Learning objective
Knowledge and
Understanding of the
World – To learn how
to operate cassette
recorders.

Group size
Individual children.

What you need
A cassette recorder, headphones if possible, cassettes of well-known stories, comfortable cushions and a quiet corner in the library.

Setting up
Talk about stories. Sometimes we read stories for ourselves, sometimes with help from other people, sometimes we have them read to us and today, we are going to listen to them on a cassette recorder.

What to do
Show the children the cassette recorder, pointing out the buttons and what they all do. Have a special place for cassettes on a shelf in the library. Show how to load a cassette and how to press the 'play' button to begin the story. Explain how they can press 'pause' if they want to stop the story for a moment and how to press 'stop' when they have come to the end. If the story is recorded on two sides, demonstrate how they should remove the cassette – the 'eject' button – and reload the other side. If the cassette recorder operates from the mains, talk about the wire and plug and the on/off switch. (CARE!) Make it clear that only adults should attempt to plug in or unplug the recorder. The children should be allowed to switch the recorder on and off at the switch, under supervision. If your recorder has a light showing that it is on, point this out to the children. Provide a set of headphones if possible. Explain their operation to the children.

Questions to ask
How do we turn the recorder on? How do we start the story? How do I stop it? Why are we using headphones?

For younger children
In order to hold younger children's interest, choose stories which have an accompanying booklet so that the children can look at pictures while they listen to the cassette.

For older children
Let these children experiment with recording their own stories on to blank cassettes. Go through how to press the 'record' and 'play' buttons together and show them how to speak into the microphone on the recorder so that their voices are heard clearly.

Follow-up activities
• Record stories for the children to listen to in the Library. Miss out certain key words so that the children have to use their imagination to fill in the gaps.
• Discuss their possible use of audio-visual equipment in their own homes. Do the buttons on these do similar things? Are any of them operated by remote control?
• Can the children think of any other electrical appliances in common use in homes which are operated by buttons or switches? (Telephones, lights and so on.)

OUR OWN BOOKS

Learning objective
Physical Development – To develop a range of manipulative skills, through making books.

Group size
Up to six children.

What you need
Card of different thickness and colours, plain and lined paper, adhesive tape, adhesive, stapler (only for use under adult supervision), string, ribbons, pencils, coloured pencils, felt-tipped pens, erasers, scissors, coloured magazines, hole punch (CARE!).

Setting up
Explain to the children that they are going to design and make their own books to add to the collection in the Library. Discuss with each group of six children what they would like their book to be about.

What to do
Having chosen a topic for their book, help them to think about what colour and shape of card would be suitable for the book's cover. For instance, if the chosen topic was 'Kings and Queens', a cover in the shape of a crown, in golden yellow, might be appropriate. Having decided upon the cover, help each child to write something for inclusion in the book, on paper the same shape as the cover. This could be part of a joint story or something experienced by them. Encourage the children to illustrate their contributions by cutting out coloured pictures from the magazines and sticking these carefully on to paper the same shape again. When all the writing and drawing is complete, collect it all and help the children to fix the pages together with the card covers, using tape, adhesive, string, ribbon or staples. Explore all these ways of fixing the pages together. Obviously, different manipulative skills are necessary for different procedures and it is important to let the children experiment with all of these.

Questions to ask
How do we put all these pages together? How can I make a hole in all these pages? How can I use this ribbon to keep the pages together?

For younger children
Use perforated computer paper, cut into different shapes, to make a zigzag book which will unfurl. Fix it to a card cover at one end, using adhesive. Again, encourage the children to cut out pictures to illustrate their work and to write a few 'words' to go with the pictures.

For older children
Encourage ideas for different types of books, including those which might have things tucked into pockets, flaps to lift up or textures to feel. Let the children come up with ideas for attaching any extras thus practising different manipulative skills.

Follow-up activities
• Make a 'rainbow' book, by writing onto short, wide pieces of paper in the colours of the rainbow. Attach them with tape, one under the other.
• Make a book out of embroidered Binca squares, sewing the resulting 'pages' together with thread.
• Make three dimensional books, sticking writing onto card and attaching the card pieces together to make solid shapes.
• Practise folding and cutting skills with the photocopiable sheet on page 64. Hang the results in the Library.

WHAT SEASON?

Learning objective
*Creative Development
– To use a range of
materials and
resources to represent
the seasons.*

Group size
Up to six children.

What you need
Pieces of A4 card in different colours, PVA adhesive, brushes, poster paint, scissors, fabric, coloured paper, a variety of collage pieces, shiny paper, ribbon and string, cotton wool, tissue paper, books about the seasons, newspaper/PVC covering.

Setting up
Work together, look at the books showing the different seasons. Cover the tables with newspaper or PVC covering. Give each child a small pot of adhesive, a brush and a pair of scissors. Spread out the various collage materials on another table nearby so that the children can help themselves.

What to do
Explain that you are going to ask the children to produce collage pictures to represent the different seasons of the year. Encourage imaginative use of the different materials and resources. Look carefully at colours and textures which could be used to represent things seen in the spring, summer, autumn or winter. Ideas for spring could include tissue blossom, cotton wool lambs, thin green ribbon as new shoots; for summer, a painted blue and green sea, sequin flowers, green felt grass; for autumn, red, yellow and brown patterned fabric leaves, lentils as 'corn', small red beads as berries; for winter, thick pale blue paint and cling film as puddles, white felt and glitter as frost and snow and spaghetti as bare trees.

Use the resulting pictures to decorate a corner of the Library where you can make a display of books connected with the seasons.

Questions to ask
What do you see when you think about the winter? What does the sky look like when it is hot outside? Which colours make us feel hot and cold?

For younger children
Concentrate on making a sun to represent summer, using warm colours of paint and as many different collage materials as possible. Similarly, use a range of materials and resources to represent the rain and snow of winter.

For older children
Encourage more detail in the pictures, including suitable background skies.

Follow-up activities
• Referring to books in the Library, talk about the smells, sounds and tastes of the different seasons, such as the taste of newly-ripened apples.
• Use different musical instruments to represent the different seasons. For example, a tambourine could be shaken to suggest walking along a sandy beach in the summer; a triangle could suggest steps taken on a frosty walk in the snow.
• Encourage movement to a variety of music. Can they move around like autumn leaves being blown in the wind?
• Play a guessing game. Tape sounds, such as the bleating of lambs and ask the children to identify the season when they hear them.

CHAPTER EIGHT

A project about toys is always a popular choice with young children. All children have a knowledge and enthusiasm for toys, and as such, have a great deal to contribute. Establish the setting of a Toy Shop with the ideas on page 9 to make an exciting environment in which the children can play and develop skills. In this chapter there are ideas based on this theme that explore balance using see-saws, dressing-up in clothes from different cultures and moving like toys to a variety of instruments.

LET ME SHOW YOU

Learning objective
Language and Literacy – To use a growing vocabulary to express thoughts and convey meaning.

Group size
Whole group.

What you need
The children's own toys – one for each child.

Setting up
Sit all the children round in a big circle, making sure that they can all see what each child will be showing them.

What to do
Ask each child in turn to describe their toy. Tell them to hold the toy up high so that all the children can see and (if they are happy for this to happen) then pass it round so that everyone can touch and examine it for themselves. Make sure that other children listen carefully to those who are talking to the group. Test understanding from time to time by asking specific children to repeat what has been said.
It may be necessary to prompt the 'describers' from time to time by suggesting other things to say. For example, can the children say what their toy is made out of, and how it works?

Questions to ask
Who gave you this toy? Does it have a name? What makes it move? Was it a present for a special occasion? Have you ever lost it? How did you feel then?

For younger children
Ask these children specific questions about their toys, rather than asking them to describe their toys without any prompting. Try to use open-ended questions, for example, 'Tell me how your toy moves', rather than those which require one-word answers, such as 'Is this your favourite toy?'.

For older children
Encourage as much detail as possible in the descriptions you are being offered. Help the children to improve their vocabulary, by asking them to repeat a simple sentence using more adjectives. For example; 'My doll is pretty' could become 'My princess doll is wearing a pink dress with stars on it and silver shoes. She is pretty.'

Follow-up activities
• Set up a display of the toys which have been brought in. Make sure that children understand the need for great care when handling these toys.
• Ask children to talk about their own birthdays and their experiences of receiving presents on these days.
• Read the children a simple story. Assess how well they have listened by asking them to repeat the story in their own words.

UP, DOWN OR LEVEL?

Learning objective
Mathematics – To compare the weights of different objects using balance scales and a see-saw (CARE!).

Group size
Up to eight children.

What you need
Balance scales, a see-saw. A selection of small items, for example, real 1p coins, plastic counting bricks, feathers, paper, pencils, marbles (CARE!), small bouncy balls, toy cars. Dolls and soft toys.

Setting up
Spread out all the small objects on the table and set up the balance scales within easy reach. Arrange the see-saw, together with a few large dolls and soft toys, in a corner of the room and do not let children experiment without adult supervision.

What to do
Explain how toys in the Toy Shop can be used to conduct some simple comparative experiments about the weight of different objects and materials. Explore together what it means when the balance remains level or tips to one side or the other. Working in pairs, let the children choose two objects from the selection. Ask them to guess which is heavier and let them check by trying for themselves, using the balance scales. Having observed what happens, encourage them to make sensible guesses as to the number of feathers they will need in order to balance one plastic brick, for example. Again, let them check their answers with the scales.

Then move on to the see-saw. Start by choosing two children of roughly equal weight. Make sure each child sits right at the end of the see-saw. Observe how the see-saw remains level. Next, ask another child to sit close to one already on the see-saw and watch as that end goes down. Ask the children to try to make the see-saw level again, in whatever way they can.

Questions to ask
What does it mean when this end of the scales/see-saw goes down? Which is heavier/lighter? How many of these weigh the same as one of those? Which material is this made of? Are plastic or metal toy cars heavier?

For younger children
Use balance scales only and work with slightly larger objects.

For older children
Pre-balance the see-saw by choosing two children of similar weight and then make it into a 'human balance' by giving each child a large basket. Let the children experiment with the different weights of dolls and soft toys by placing these in the baskets. Again, encourage guesses first. Are these right?

Follow-up activities
• Using toys from the Toy Shop, can the children find three objects lighter/heavier than a Teddy, without weighing them?
• Ask the children to help you arrange the Toy Shop, taking account of the weight of the toys. Are shelves strong enough? Where can we put very heavy items?
• Ask the children to sort a collection of toy animals by weight, from the lightest to the heaviest.
• Use as much mathematical language as posssible, such as, how many more/less and put another in/ take one out.

LET'S PRETEND

Learning objective
Personal and Social Development – To develop an understanding of and respect for people of other cultures.

Group size
Up to six children.

What you need
A selection of dressing-up items including jackets and trousers, thick coats and furry hoods, saris and cholis, dresses, kimonos, striped cotton tunics, belts, sashes, hats, headsquares, head-dresses and veils. Also, some multicultural puzzles and books, face paints, tissue or crêpe paper, needle and wool, cushions, poster paints, crayons and felt-tipped pens, paper and card, Christmas decorations.

Setting up
Explain that you would like the children to take it in turns to wear some of the different dressing-up clothes.

What to do
Examine the books and do the puzzles together to gain some knowledge of the kind of clothing worn by people from other cultures. Let the children explore the available clothing and try it on for themselves. Encourage children who know how these clothes are worn to share their expertise with the group as a whole. Compare the different types of clothing. Let the children indulge in imaginative play in their new identities, again taking ideas from the books or puzzles or from children of the same culture. Children wearing Indian clothes could paint patterns on their hands and make and wear paper garlands as they dance in celebration of the coming of spring, or Holi. Similarly, those in Japanese dress might have a pretend meal at a very low table while sitting on cushions on the floor as they would in an authentic Japanese home. Children wearing the tunics, belts and veils of North Africa might like to decorate cards and wrapping paper with geometric patterns to wrap up presents to take to their friends at a pretend party in celebration of Eid-ul Fitr. Children dressed in European clothes could visit the Toy Shop which has been specially decorated as Father Christmas's Grotto.

Questions to ask
Why do you think this type of dress is worn in this part of the world? Why are loose clothes worn where it is very hot? What does it feel like wearing a sari?

For younger children
Try to gather together a collection of dolls from around the world. Show these to the children so that they can see the different costumes. (Pictures from magazines are a good second best). Then let them try the clothes on for themselves.

For older children
Ask the children to try creating their own saris, kimonos and tunics from large pieces of fabric. Can this just be draped around the children's bodies?

Follow-up activities
• Compare patterns seen on fabric in this country with those found in other areas of the world. Glossy magazines provide a good source of photographs.
• Identify clothes worn in hot and cold areas of the world. Look at the textures and weights of the fabrics.
• Try to find a video to watch of genuine celebratory events around the world.

HIT THE KEYS!

Learning objective
Knowledge and
Understanding of the
World – To learn how
to operate a computer
by using the arrow
keys or mouse with
software involving
games.

Group size
One child at a time.

What you need
A computer with suitable software and a comfortable chair. The software could involve simple sorting, matching or sequencing games, pattern making or activities such as dressing Teddy.

Setting up
Make sure the child is comfortable and can easily reach all the computer controls.

What to do
Assume the child has never used a computer before (some may well have done but they may not have used the same make or the same kind of mouse). Load software which works with either arrow keys or a mouse. If the children are using arrow keys, help them to connect the arrow direction with the way they want their person or thing to move. If the programme is mouse-operated, show the children how to hold the mouse correctly. For their purposes, the only button they will need to press will be the left-hand one. Help them to practise doing this without touching anything else on the mouse. Now practise moving the arrow around the screen slowly. When they are reasonably competent at this, practise 'picking up' items by clicking on them once. When they are where the children want them to be, click again to 'drop' them.

Questions to ask
Are you holding the mouse correctly? Which finger should you press down? Which way do you want to go? Have you ever played this game before? Was it on a computer or were you using cards on a table?

For younger children
Use 'arrow' key operated software or that which requires very simple mouse movements, perhaps lifting only one item from the screen. If possible, choose games which make use of smiley faces when the children match things correctly or those which use 'happy' and 'sad' sounds for right and wrong answers.

For older children
Help these children to load their own software, selecting from a choice on the screen. When they have completed an exercise, show them how to remove it and bring up a new screen, by clicking on the appropriate symbols.

Follow-up activities
• Try a selection of software with each child to find exercises which both stimulate and excite each individual child.
• Assess how the children rate the computer as a toy. Do they enjoy playing on it?
• Examine the computer keyboard and show children what happens on the screen when they press individual letters on the keyboard. Explain that it can be used instead of a pencil for writing.
• Explain how to switch the computer on and off correctly. This should always be done under adult supervision.

WHAT AM I?

Learning objective
Physical Development – To encourage children to move imaginatively and confidently with increasing control and co-ordination.

Group size
Whole group.

What you need
A large room so that children can move around freely, the sounds of several instruments including triangles, glockenspiels, wood blocks, various drums, guiros, tambourines, maracas, duck calls and so on.

Setting up
Ask the children to spread out, find a space in the room and sit down.

What to do
Play each instrument and ask the children to identify which toy each sound suggests. For example, the tinkling sound of glockenspiels might suggest fairy dolls, beaten drums – toy soldiers and short duck calls – bouncing balls. Decide together which instrument suggests which toy and then explain to the children that you will play the different instruments in turn. When they hear the right sound for each toy, you want them to move around the room, in time to the different instruments, imitating the movements of that toy. Watch to see how the children are interpreting the sounds and be ready to offer suggestions. Give the children a chance to develop and explore their own ideas.

Questions to ask
How do soldiers march along? If you were a fairy doll in a beautiful dress, how would you move? What does this sound make you think of? Can you think of something else which makes this sort of sound?

For younger children
Let these children use some dressing-up clothes to help them get 'in role' and therefore to move more appropriately.

For older children
Suggest that they try to co-ordinate some of their movements with a partner. Encourage them to perform their 'dance' to the rest of the group. Allow them to use the instruments.

Follow-up activities
• Using some of the toys as props, help the children to mime how they would feel receiving such a toy from a friend.
• Act out the job of a toy-maker together. Pretend to be sawing wood, hammering, painting, polishing and sewing.
• Have a session moving around an obstacle course set out in a large area. Use a selection of items from the Toy Shop such as hoops, balls and skipping ropes.

CAN I PLAY?

Learning objective
Creative Development
– To develop
imaginative play with
table-top toys.

Group size
Three different groups
of two children.

What you need
Several table-top toys from the Toy Shop, such as a doll's house (complete with furniture) and a play family, a garage with toy cars and road signs and a farm with animals, fencing, tractors, farm workers and a farm house.

Setting up
Clear a large space on the floor or use a large table-top. Lay out the doll's house, garage and farm allowing plenty of room for two children to play comfortably around each one.

What to do
Allow the children to play freely, using their own ideas and imagination. Give them suggestions for extending the scope of their play if necessary. For example, you might suggest that the family decide to re-arrange some of the rooms in their house or make preparations for a new baby. When playing with the garage, pretend that one of the cars has broken down while out on the roadway they have created. On the farm, the farmer could be taking the cows in from the fields for milking. When the children are playing happily and the ideas are flowing easily, sit back and observe them as they use their own imaginations to continue the play. Do any children take on specific roles? Who are the leaders?

Questions to ask
Why do we use a garage? Which animals would you expect to find on a farm? If you had this house, which room would be your bedroom?

For younger children
Read suitable stories, for example: *Five Minutes Peace* and *A Piece of Cake* by Jill Murphy (Walker) and *Mr Gumpy's Outing* by John Burningham (Picture Puffin). These will encourage the children to think themselves into the parts and therefore to play co-operatively.

For older children
Use toys such as DUPLO and LEGO so that the children have to make their own houses, cars, trees, walls and so on before they use them for play, thus making the exercise more challenging.

Follow-up activities
• Use play dough of different consistencies and modelling clay and make objects to add to the play accessories for the house, farm and garage.
• Give children play money from the Toy Shop and see how they can incorporate its use into their play. They could perhaps buy food for their family, buy petrol at the garage or pay for dairy products from the farm.
• Use other toys from the Toy Shop, such as dolls and Teddy bears to encourage more imaginative play.

PHOTOCOPIABLES

Name _____

Can you repeat these patterns?

Name _____

Colour things which go in the air – blue,
things which go in the water – green and
those which go on the ground – red.

Name _____

fur	ears	paws	nose	claws	whiskers

Name _____

Draw a line from this boy to each item he needs to stay healthy.

Name _____

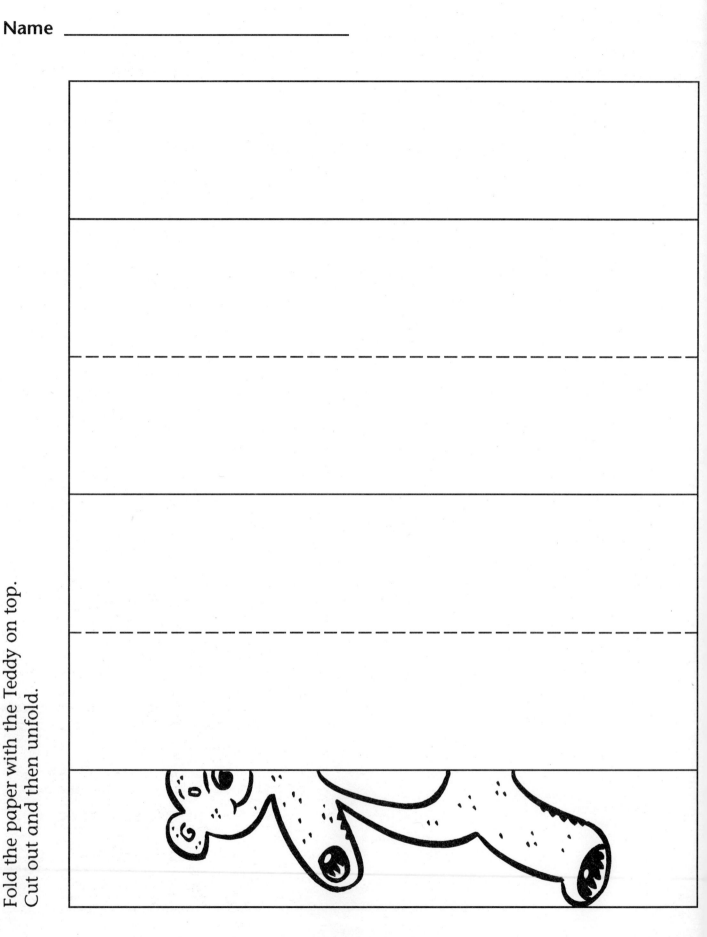

Fold the paper with the Teddy on top.
Cut out and then unfold.